Very Truly Yours

Ginny Nickoloff

All rights reserved. No part of this book may be used or reproduced in any manner whatsoever without written permission except in the case of brief quotations embodied in crucial articles and reviews.

Copyright © 2024 Virginia Nickoloff

ISBN 13: 978-1-951543-31-0

DANCING CROWS
PRESS

Dancingcrowspress@gmail.com

Printed in the United States of America

Dedication

May my great grandchildren Avery, Natalie, Clementine, Maxtone and Teddy have some love for history and family values in a more perfect world.

Chapter One

I'm writing this book about letters before letters are extinct and no one knows what I'm talking about. I'm 99 years old and stubbornly refusing to get a cell phone, primarily because I see everyone with a cellphone in their face, existing in some other world. A friend of mine has a basket by her front door for her family to deposit their cellphones before they enter.

There are letters of the alphabet, the letter of the law, business letters, thank-you notes, cheery notes from home, wish you were here, picture post cards, love letters when hearts are separated from each other.

I still pay my bills with a check. Companies are so mad at me that they don't even enclose a return envelope anymore. Are post offices and mailmen going to become extinct?

I understand that cursive writing (long hand) is not being taught in school anymore and time is told in digital instead of a clock face. Poor Big Ben is only telling time for older London residents.

UPDATE: I've just received an email from son Jac telling me that California has just passed a law saying the schools must teach cursive writing starting January 2024. Hooray!!!

One can save things on a cellphone, but for how long? I saved a column written by Ellen Goodman, a columnist for the Boston Globe in 1985 comparing phone calls to letters. Her last paragraph: "But you cannot hold a call in your hands. You cannot put it in a bundle. You cannot show it to your family. Indeed, there is nothing to show for it. It doesn't leave a trace. Tell me how can you wrap a lifetime of phone calls in a rubber band for a summer's night when you want to remember?"

Letters written by famous people become valuable as witnessed by a tender and touching letter that author John Steinbeck penned to his teenage son, offering fatherly advice after the young man confided that he was in love for the first time (then 14 years old). The letter written in 1958 was up for auction expecting to get a big price.

Do children exchange Valentines at school anymore? My mother saved a valentine she received from Waldo in 1910. She was six years old.

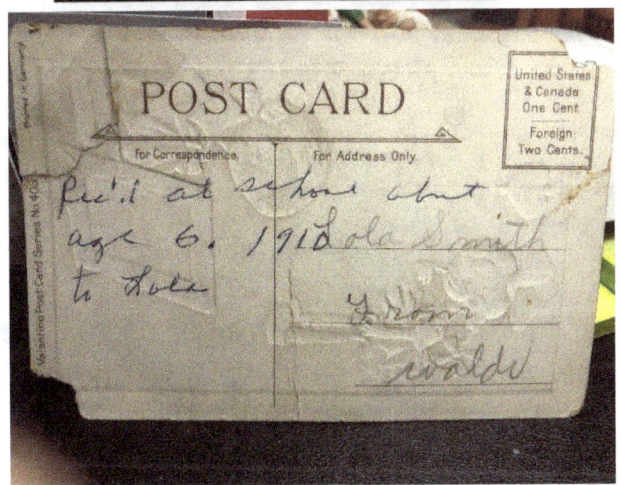

Notice on the back of the Valentine the stamp was one cent in the U.S. & Canada and Foreign two cents. A far-cry from the cost of postage today.

My husband made a Valentine for me in 1986 that touched my heart. I saved it under glass on my nightstand.

I was a business major in high school, taking shorthand, typing and business math. These cartoons made me laugh:

I still use shorthand to catch the words of a song on the radio or take quick notes. Gregg shorthand was taught all over the world. Court reporters recorded the court proceedings in shorthand until electronic recorders took their place. Here is a sample of shorthand:

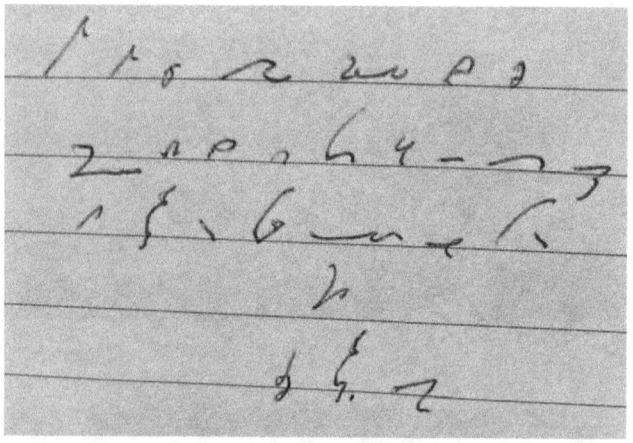

The translation:

Dear Sir,

It is with great sorrow that we inform you that your book was not good enough to publish. Better luck next time.

Very truly yours,
Cheezy Publishing Company

Chapter Two

I met my husband on a blind date in Los Angeles during World War II. My girlfriend Marlyn called to see if I could go with her, her boyfriend Art and his cousin Jim to a movie. We went to see Mickey Rooney in "Double Trouble".

After the movie, we went to Art's house. He made pancakes and then played records and we danced. I called my mom at 1:30 a.m. and told her I'd be home pretty soon. Jimmy in his Navy Air Force uniform cocked his officer's cap on the back of his head and my heart did flip flops. He drove me home and, usually shy, I bit the bullet and asked him if he would like my address. He wrote it down on a slip of paper and many years later I discovered he still had it in his wallet.

Jimmy left the next day for Corpus Christi to continue his training to be a fighter pilot and land on carriers. We did not see each other again for two years when the war finally ended. We corresponded all that time and I saved all his letters. We did exchange photographs.

I was ecstatic over what he wrote on his picture.

Here is the first letter that Jimmy wrote to me showing his inimitable handwriting, making a circle for a dot over the i.

Here is a copy of the letter so you can read it easily, the envelope postmarked: June 8, 1944

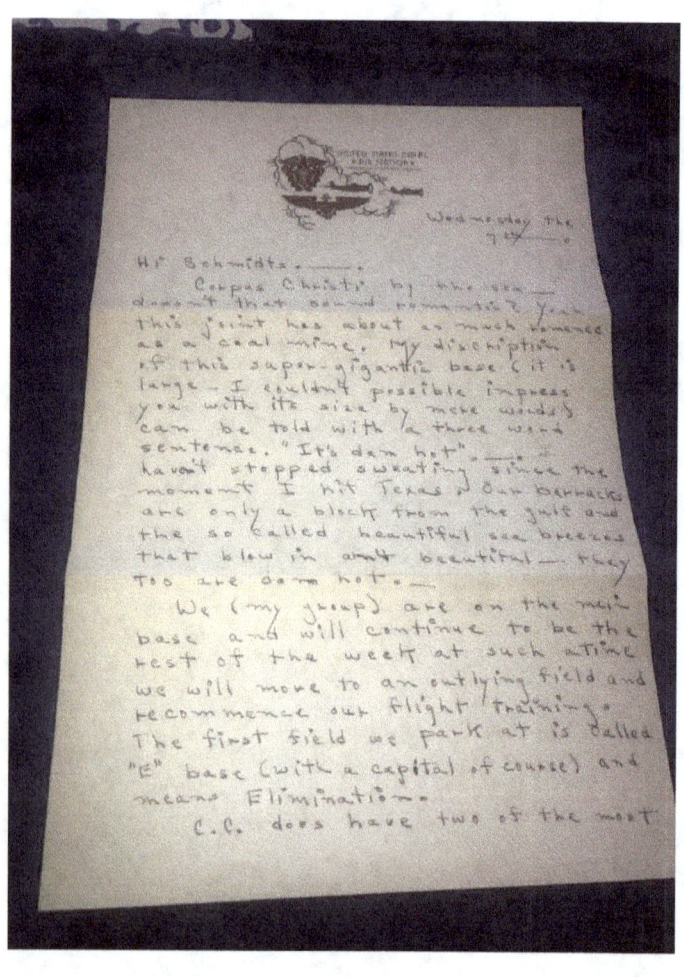

Wednesday the 7th

Hi Schmidts

Corpus Christi by the sea…. doesn't that sound romantic? Yeah, this joint has about as much romance as a coal mine. My description of this super gigantic base (it is large—I couldn't possibly impress you with its size by mere words) can be told with a three-word sentence. "It's damn hot". I haven't stopped sweating since the moment I hit Texas. Our barracks are only a block from the Gulf and the so-called beautiful sea breezes that blow in ain't beautiful—they too are damn hot.

We (my group) are on the main base and still continue to be the rest of the week at such a time we will move to an outlying field and recommence our flight training. The first field we park at is called "E" base (with a capital of course) and means Elimination.

C.C. does have two of the most lovely swimming pools. Lovely because the only other recreational facilities we have are tennis and handball—both of which if played in this weather for twenty minutes would cause me to lose twenty pounds. (All right so the doc did say I was twenty-three pounds overweight—his scales are phooey) I'd look skinny at 160#). I should get *one hell of a tan with the amount of swimming I've been getting in. I imagine the weather is a poor subject to discuss, but honestly the damn heat (and of course, girls) are the only "things" we ourselves can think about.*

It was a bit dark when you gave me your photo and consequently not being able to see it, I didn't get a chance to tell you how very much I like it. But then, It's of you and you're sorta pretty (I mean the fellows like your picture), and I do miss you. I'm sorry I don't have a small photo to give you in return. The snap enclosed is about the best I can do. If anything, it flatters me. Write sorta soon! Jim

As an example, I received five letters in July of 1944, so I have a whole box of letters Jimmy wrote to me. We were married 53 years and every anniversary we would pull out a letter and read it.

Jimmy passed away before the dawn of 2000.

Unbelievably, I recently received the following letter dated March 10, 1960, from Jimmy's cousin Art's sister. Art was the cousin who died very young which prompted Jimmy to have family reunions.

Dear Ginny,

I've been wanting to get this to you since I first found it at my mom's house (years ago). Jim wrote it to Art after your first date, but unfortunately the first page of it has disappeared, so no date.

The letter head:
OTTUMWA,
NAVAL AIR STATION

"...has a plane and two cadets fly wing on him for an hour and a half—that's the length of the periods. That gives us a nice three plane formation. Most of the period is spent in a V formation. We usually fly two periods a day which is plenty.

Hey, Chum, I want to thank you and Marlyn for the swell time on that date we had, but even more, I want to thank you for "the date."

Boy, that Ginny is quite a gal. Man alive, I fell madly in love with her the first time I saw her. I have written her twice and received one letter from her. It's her time to write now. Boy, what a gal!

Well, Art, guess I'll close now, and I'll probably be hearing from you soon, huh?

Your cousin,

Jim

You can imagine how thrilled I was to receive this letter 40 years later and know that we both fell in love at the same time.

By 1945, Jimmy was back in California as he was stationed in Indio, but I was a hundred miles away in Yosemite. Soon he shipped out from San Francisco to Hawaii to join his fighter Flight Group VF13. I received seventeen more letters with the return address: Ensign J.A. Nickoloff, VF98, c/o Fleet Post Office, San Francisco, Calif.

The location of every service man in World War II was secret, but the War Office knew where each one was and managed to get mail delivered to all parts of the world and aboard ships and submarines eventually. Lucky for Jimmy, the war

ended in August of 1945, and he was spared from actual combat duty.

By October 1945, he was released from the Navy, and I was home from Yosemite.

My two friends, Marilyn and Kris and I had enrolled at the University of Southern California in September of 1945. Jimmy took me to a Hollywood nightclub and proposed marriage.

I showed my friends my engagement ring and quit U.S.C. after one semester. I applied and got a job working for a law firm (Boyle, Holms, Frye and Garrett) to earn money for my trousseau. I was finally using my high school skills, shorthand and typing, as I was the switch-board operator, receptionist and took dictation.

Jimmy's first love was baseball. He was catcher and pitcher with some local teams in Los Angeles and signed with the Cleveland Indians reporting to spring training in Bakersfield. I thought I was going to be a baseball wife.

His first letter from the Bakersfield Padre Hotel dated April 15, 1946:

Hello my darling,

I really haven't a thing to tell (except that I love you) and I am only writing because I want to hear from you. Seems in order to fill up this sheet I'll relate some of the uneventful happenings that have taken place.

 First, we arrived yesterday afternoon and promptly had dinner. Then after a short "hello" speech, a couple of the fellows and I took in one of the local movies. This morning 'bout ten –spring training began and, Oh my Gawd—millions of men all over the field. The team can carry only fifteen men—so I reckon about thirty of us will be returning home—soon.

 Not a great deal took place today, a little batting and fielding practice for almost five hours. The weather, never to be forgotten, is hot but good for our needs (they tell me). I imagine in a few days we will play a few games among ourselves, then a bit of elimination, then some more exhibition games. The story should be told very shortly.

 Been thinking for ten minutes just now and I guess nothing else happened today. So-o-o g'nite for now my darling.

      oo-oo I love you,
      Your Jimmy

The Sunday before Jimmy left for Bakersfield, he played in two "pick-up" games in Los Angeles—pitching one game and catching the second one. He hadn't been working out in the Navy and after a few days in Bakersfield, his arm gave out and he dejectedly returned home.

At that time, California had no professional baseball teams. Jimmy told me that he wanted to go to New York to see the Yankees play. He would be gone six months. With $12 in his pocket, his friend drove him to the outskirts of Los Angeles where he could hitch a ride. I received the following letter from New York:

Willian Sloan House
New York City's Y.M.C.A. for
Transient Young Men
356 West 34th Street
New York 1, N.Y.

May 9, 1946

My Darling,

Long time no see, no speak, no hear, no nothing—the state of this union is awful. I finally arrived to my destination late last evening—"Noo Yawk" and little girl, this is a wonderful town—just millions of people running wild. The first thing I did today was take off for Yankee Stadium and after all these years, saw my first major league ball game—s'wonderful.

I reckon I'd better jump back a couple of weeks and give the first report of my journey. I did leave L.A. the next day, the 24th of April—by the "next day" I mean right after our last date.

This traveling by the thumb method gets rather "rugged" at times and if I can help it, I'll never do it again. My first ride took me as far as San Bernardino, then, right off the bat, I caught another one within fifty miles of Phynix (sp?) Arizona. I got there about ten in the evening and along came my first rough night. Then hours later, I got a ride to a little past Phynix (I don't know how to spell it) This fellow dropped me off right by a little civilian airport—guess what—I spent two dollars for an airplane ride!

The next ride wasn't too hot, but at last I was moving —slow but sure—after two days—we crossed most of Texas and landed in Houston—he "let me drive" most of the nights so after three days with hardly any sleep, I passed out in a hotel room in Houston for about eighteen hours.

Feeling fine and happy with the world once again, I hit the road and everything was fine— 'till I got half-way through Louisiana where I stood fourteen hours trying to catch a ride. I finally did and got as far as Mobile, Alabama. Right about here my funds gave out. (Guess I should have taken more than the twelve bucks that were in my pocket.) But times as they are and jobs plentiful, I had no difficulty washing dishes for a few days.

Arriving in Jax Fla still low on the green stuff, I soda jerked in a drug store for six days—a slight improvement over my first job. Being so near "that place" took off for it and arrived before noon—just nice so I could spend nearly a whole day on the beach. That evening I headed out for my destination (N.Y. of course) and here I am.

I've got my room rent paid up for a week and I figure I won't have to work again until Monday if I eat lightly—then I'll be able to attend every game of this coming Red Sox-Yank series at Yankee Stadium—which promises to be one fine series—the Red Sox at present are leading the league and I understand they have a real pennant team.

I reckon it's about closing time Honey Chile. I sure have missed you little girl and I sure do love you. This life is ok but Darling I'm so lonesome for you. Write me soon and keep them coming.

All my love darling, Jimmy

At the foot of the stationery:

1493 FIREPROOF ROOMS—RATES 75¢ $1.00 A DAY AND UP

BATHS - RESTAURANT- GYMNASUM – BILLIARDS

PERSONAL COUNSELING AND EMPLOYMENT SERVICE

DAILY PROGRAM OF ACTIVITIES-RECREATON INFO

Again, on the Y.M.C.A. stationery, a letter dated 29, May 1946:

My Darling,

From the text of your last letter, I take it you're somewhat put out over the state of my correspondence—and considering that I've written but one letter to date—it is quite just that you should feel as you do. So, with the writing of this letter and my most humble apologies, everything should be fine and dandy once again.

I should have remembered that things are pretty tough for you. You still live with your folks—you see them every day and by your other letters, I see your friends have been neglecting you (the beach trips and those awful mountains) and then you have the awful streetcar situation to contend with—yes, I should have remembered!

But enough of this idle chatter—you would like to know what I've been doing—so you can tell your friends and your pride won't suffer. Yes, we must maintain our pride.

Well, you know about the ball games I saw the first few days. I think it was on a Monday I went to work, must have been the thirteenth. I get off at nine o'clock in the evening and usually I take a long walk—alone. I can't hardly remember where these walks have taken me, but it never mattered cause I didn't walk to go sightseeing, but merely to pass the time somehow....it seems to hang kinda heavy—reckon I'm a little lonesome—seven million people packed like sardines and yet I could be no more alone than if I were sitting on the north pole.

That's all I've been doing—just a working and a walking—no sightseeing—haven't been up on top the Empire State Building, haven't been to Brooklyn—haven't danced, haven't gotten drunk, haven't done a damn thing.

I'm still here at the Y.M.C.A. and again, I haven't written to <u>anyone</u> more than I've written to you, so quit your crying and get <u>tough</u>. That's the first lesson I learned, no one in New York feels sorry for me and I haven't time to feel sorry for you--even if I <u>thought</u> I should.

Your Brat

*P.S. Tho seemingly I wander
aimlessly
Our love keeps me ever
on the straight and true
road.
Jimmy*

I cringed when I read this balling out that he gave me!

Jimmy's original intention was to stay six months in New York, but after three months he was ready to come home. He hitchhiked as far as Texas and called his Dad to send money for a flight home. When he called me, I had just washed my hair. Personal hair dryers hadn't been invented yet. A girl's biggest problem has always been fixing and maintaining her hairdo. Ask any female from age 10 to 100. I panicked!

I was still working at the law office and my Mom was busy making my wedding gown, bridesmaids' gowns, flower girls' dresses and her own gown illustrated in the picture below, not to mention my trousseau. The wedding date was set for Sunday, February 16, 1947.

Jimmy's best friend in the Navy was Bernie Meyers. When Jimmy came home from Hawaii and was discharged from the Navy, Bernie stayed in the Navy in Hawaii and he got in a fight and received a blow to the jaw. Jimmy and I visited him at the Naval hospital in San Diego and then he was sent to New York. The following letter was postmarked Brooklyn, New York with the address:

Lt (jg) B. Meyers
USN Hosp
Brooklyn, NY, 24 Jan '47

Dear Ginny,

Have been thinking of you quite a bit since your epistle of Nov. 5. I'm real happy for you, gal, and you've got. my best wishes with you whenever you feel you'll need 'em .

Never underestimate the power of a woman--that's really something to get Jimmy boy talkin' about refrigerators and stuff—but I do believe you two have the right thing—you've stammered and stalled enough to know your own minds by this time and that's just as it should be.

My heart aches to be there when you two splice the knot and a few weeks ago I had visions of making it—but since then the Navy has pulled up somethin' terrific and now I don't see how it can be done—but please know that if I can possibly make it, I'll be there to kiss the bride! That's worth a trip across two continents-- but as I said the success of such a dream is shrouded in damp, sticky darkness but I'll be there in spirit anyhoo wishin' you two all the luck at my command—and according to the medics around here, that's something I have plenty of!!

Speaking of me, I'm doin' great--even carrying on a romance here and there myself! Didn't think it could be done with half the upper jaw missin'! Most of the upper lip is numb too, but it works surprisingly well and gettin' better all the time--wonderful thing, exercise!

Regards to Mom and Pop and much happiness to V. Schmidt, Chief!

Love, Bernie

P.S. If I'm not there be sure and have a dance for me! Bernie

This heartbreaking letter was the last we heard from Bernie. Since we named our first son James Bernard after Bernie, Jimmy stayed in touch with Bernie's folks in Chicago and one year, we invited them to come visit and go to the Rose Parade—-the only time we ever paid for seats.

Jimmy loved to fly friends to Catalina Island. One Sunday we were flying back with our friends, Nick and Betty Argy, coming in for a landing, the plane's radio said, "Check fire on left wing." Betty and I froze in the back seat. Actually, it was a fire on the ground!

Here is a postcard Jimmy sent me on one of his visits to Catalina:

We celebrated our 50th anniversary in Atlanta with all the family giving speeches and then we all went to Johnny's Hideaway for dancing.

Chapter Three

I turned 21 on August 25, 1945, while I was working in Yosemite with my friends Marilyn, Kris and Marlyn. We called ourselves the "Four Jewels."

Ginny, Marilyn, Kris, and Marlyn

The few days we four Jewels spent in Yosemite on our vacation in 1944 inspired us to apply for spring jobs at the cafeteria in March. Those few weeks we tried skiing for the first time. Then we were determined to get summer jobs in 1945. This is probably the first letter I wrote to my folks with a Camp Curry dateline June 1, 1945:

Dear Mom and Daddy:

Golly, I just don't know where to begin—but anyway—coming into the valley just knocked me out again. It is completely changed from the winter scenery. There are tiny falls coming down all over the glacier cliffs and Yosemite Falls is just loaded with water.

This winter the trees were leafless and now they are just gorgeous, the most beautiful chartreuse green you can imagine. Some of them have great big white flowers like dogwood. The meadows too green to be real.

Well, to get on with the story. Terry had reserved a tent for us facing theirs. It's on the **cool** *"terrace" but seems more like the alps. When we saw it—we thought we would go back to L.A. The sum total is a 9 x 12 tent with a wood floor, two dressers—only one with a mirror, two tables and a* big wood box Terry had found for us—two iron beds. Man, were we sad! But we decided that other people can take it so--. The next day we reported and neither of us had to go to work, so we really dug in and made the place a home. And if we do say so ourselves, it's the niftiest tent in the place.

The funny thing is—everything is so handy—in bed I can reach almost anything I want. My drawers just have room to open and that's all. We put a broom handle across a corner to hang our clothes on. It fell down three times before we finally got it fixed.

Yesterday it hailed—can you imagine! Our dear tent doesn't close—the flaps have shrunk or something. We discovered today that someone has written her name on the flap with 1928 after it so you can bet this tent is at least 20 years old. I'm surprised it hangs together at all.

Well, anyway, last night I wrote a letter to Jimmy and I sat in bed with my beach towel over me, flannels on, my green robe on, a wool scarf around my neck and we had the flap pinned all the way down. We stayed warm all night so guess that's the way we sleep from now on.

Of all things, the plumber has been messing with the water and we haven't had hot water since we've been here—(no showers). Betty and Pat came down tonight and said they were organizing a group to go smelling arm pits!!!

(We had to climb a hill to the club house to go to the bathroom, shower, and wash our clothes. Mom spoiled me so bad. I had never washed or ironed before! I was trying to iron a blouse with buttons down the front. This girl waiting for the iron got so mad at me, she grabbed the iron and finished my blouse.)

Thursday---Golly what a day. I started working at nine this morning scrubbing the tables and chairs in the dining room, getting ready for the big opening tomorrow night. Boy, do I have the job—everyone acts as though I'm a queen or something to have gotten such a deal. The rest of those poor kids work like dogs.

We had about three practices today seating imaginary guests and the kids served a whole meal just like they would really. We hostesses have our own private table right up front where we are <u>served</u> our own dinner when the guests are all in. Just like we were guests every night.

I suppose you know the news about Kris and Sunnie coming in next week as hostesses, too!

(My bedmate, Marlyn worked in the gift shop. This is the same Marlyn that was on the double date when I met Jimmy. She had married Jimmy's cousin Art Nickoloff in the meantime, and he was overseas in a submarine somewhere in the Pacific.)

We got the call from Kris this afternoon so we started looking for some tents for them and we found three **new** *tents way up on a hill they call "Deerlick" so we quickly go down and see if we can change so all six of us can be together.*

Well, tonight we started moving. It was just like climbing Half Dome in the dark, back and forth, stumble stumble, but it sure is worth it—so we have moved from "Wilting Heights" to the "Schmidtkoloff Chateau". Doesn't that sound French?

Golly, this place is heaven, the flap closes without pins and it's white so we can see each other without straining our eyes. We bought a 2-bit glass fruit bowl that really classes up the joint. I have 19 cents to live on until the 22nd, but I can do it up here.

All my love, Ginny
Love for Wooley, too. (my cat)

My parents sent me a birthday card and my Mom included a six-page letter written on one side and my Dad wrote six pages on the other side.

My Mom told me about the day I was born in Orange County Hospital in Santa Ana, California. She said my dad wanted to watch, but he fainted.

I must have told them that I had an alcoholic drink legally for the first time because in my dad's letter he cautioned me about alcoholism. He always called me Snooks. I would say my prayers and he would kiss me goodnight and say, "Sleep tight and don't let the bedbugs bite!"

My Dad was manager of a large commercial laundry, hence the comments in the following letter dated June 13, 1945:

Dear Mom, Daddy, Wooley,

Monday, - washday - and I just finished my washing: 5 blouses, a slip, 2 brassieres, 8 panties, 8 prs. sox and I washed last Monday, too. Pretty soon I can tell you, Daddy, how this washing business can be run more smoothly!!

(My job in Yosemite was hostess in the Curry Dining Room...greeting people and seating them. My hours were from 8-9 am, 12 noon to 1 pm. and 6 to

8 pm. Our board and room (a tent) were included. We actually received $20 cash every two weeks.)

My letter continues:

We had another quaint weekend. More foreigners from the United Nations Peace Conference in San Francisco. The ones that drove us nuts are from Persia. The homeliest men I've ever seen and about 10 of them!

One was wandering around the dining room, and I asked him if he'd like to be seated and eat so he says "Your beautiful face astounds my friends. I would like your face for breakfast, lunch and dinner." He said he would ask the manager if I could have lunch with him, so I very definitely told him it was impossible.

As if that wasn't bad enough, he waves across the dining room and calls me over to have my picture taken in front of his people. My face must have looked like a beet. They kept insisting and making such a hub bub that I finally consented to step out front and have it taken--all of them trying to get in the picture with me. It must have been wearing that yellow dress that you made, Mom!!

I'm really getting the compliments on my clothes. Besides the waitresses telling me they always wait to see what I'll wear--the guests keep telling me how cute my clothes are. That same day I wore the yellow, a lady said "My, you have the best-looking clothes" so I told her you made most of them and her husband said you must be an accomplished woman!!

You know my $4.95 striped skirt...one morning a man asked if I'd ever been to France and if I knew such and such--a French designer because he designs clothes similarly to that. When I told him. "no"--he wanted to know if I chose my own clothes or if my mother helped me. Can you imagine my clothes having that much effect...it really amazed me.

Gee, it is really swell with all of us here now--seems to make such a difference. Kris arrived Friday night and ten of us had a party in a tent for her. Food and singing and did we ever bother everyone but nobody near us cares if you are having fun noisily cause they do it, too.

Did Johnny call you up--of all things---I had Friday off and I didn't tell him, so he looked all over for me and had to leave Friday noon. He left a box for me with Marlyn--a beautiful pair of earrings--can you imagine! I was flabbergasted, but Marlyn (worked in the Camp Curry store) said when he had been in the store before he said he wished he had a girl to buy things for, so I guess he was practicing on me.

Seems like I always have so much to tell you, but I'll write again soon. You write, okay??

All my love, Ginny

August 25, 1945
21st Birthday

Dear Mom and Daddy,

Your letters were wonderful and made me feel good all over---all 21 years of me!! I was so happy yesterday. I just hopped! You couldn't have chosen a gift I've wanted more than the sterling. (My parents started my sterling silver place settings). I just sing inside thinking about it.

The kids asked me what I'd like to do tonight and so, at my suggestion, we are having just a little party time in Sunnie's tent. An old couple that came up on the same bus with us last summer are here and they told me today was Independence

Day for me! So, the first thing I do this morning is get in a fight with some old man about toast.

We hostesses claim the title Good Samaritans of Yosemite. This last week there have been five blind soldiers here with their orientators-- three of them were officers and they were all 21 to 25.

They were the most wonderful fellows and did everything--swam, rode horses, hiked, fished, danced. They made more of a game out of it, telling milk from water by the weight, etc.

Two of them insisted on staying in a tent by themselves and one night they got all ready to go to bed and thought perhaps the light was still on--so they climbed around and finally found the bulb and unscrewed it! When they left, the whole dining room sang: For They are Jolly Good Fellows and they stood up and beamed and looked around just like they could see us. The Chaplain said that we had done wonders for them, and you could really see the difference when they left.

Tomorrow, I think eight more are coming. They are from the Dibble Institute in San Francisco. Four of the boys have plastic eyes but the other one will never be able to have them.

We girls danced with them, and each girl rode on the bus with one and described what we were seeing, Half Dome, waterfalls, lakes, meadows.

We don't know what will be happening in the next week or so. They are still debating about closing the dining room the 3rd or the 10th. We want to hike to Merced Lake a few days before coming home if we can get reservations. Sure would like to get a ride home. Why don't you buy a new car and drive up and take us home???

I'll see you in a little while. All my love,
Ginny

Before I leave Yosemite Valley, I must tell you that just outside the Camp Curry dining room was a small band shell and rows of benches. Every night there would be some kind of performance. One night even my friends and I sang a song. But the highlight was the Fire Fall. Every night, just at the moment when the sun went down, a man at the top of Glacier Point, rising thousands of feet above the valley floor, would shout "Let the fire fall!" Burning coals were pushed off making a waterfall of fire and a girl would sing "The Indian Love Call". It was so romantic! They stopped doing it in 1968 because of fire danger. Since they had been doing it since 1868, it is a shame that it has been disbanded. Obviously, the rock face made it safe.

Dateline, San Francisco September 14, 1945

Dear Mom and Daddy,

Just got our reservations for home. No Daylight available so it's the San Joaquin Daylight—it's a 14-hour trip, but the same price, so we figure we get more for our money!!

We leave at 8 Monday morning, and we'll get there at 10. I think it's better anyway cause then all our folks can meet us—otherwise we would get there too early.

Aunt Evelyn has the darlingest house. She lives way out of San Francisco, but the Greyhound bus runs right there in about 25 minutes for 15 cents and it runs until 2:30 am.

We (Marilyn, Kris and me) got here Wednesday at 5:30 and poor Bob has been footing the bills ever since. (Bob was one of Marilyn's boyfriends in the Navy stationed in San Francisco and I had known Bob in junior high school.)

Bob took us to John's 'Rendezvous' (4$ a piece for dinner) but it was out of this world, really the "works" and he seems to know what he's getting into.

Then we went to the Top of the Mark and we thought they had drawn the blinds, the fog was so thick, we couldn't see a thing, but it cleared enough to see the Bay Bridge lighted up before we left. This must be one of the most beautiful views in the world.

Yesterday, Aunt Evelyn fixed us waffles for breakfast, then we went shopping and met Bob at 2 for lunch—lunch at the Pearl Oyster House, but I had roast beef! When we got home, Aunt Evelyn had a chicken dinner for us!! Saved Bob a little money.

Got your letter and Jimmy's here. Boy, is it cold here, in daytime too. It's worse than winter at home. See you Monday night, if I don't get a chance to write again. Love, Ginny

This letter reminds me of two things. Because all our expenses were paid in Yosemite, we were each able to save about $100 in cash. Since we were freezing in San Francisco, on our shopping trip, we each bought a coat.

The other memory was the night we went to the Top of the Mark. While we were having cocktails, a group of men came in dressed in an assortment of uniforms—maybe an Army cap and a Navy jacket. They were prisoners of war just released from Japanese prison camps and brought to San Francisco by our Navy. We girls danced with them. It was like dancing with a skeleton. You never saw such a happy group!

My little family of three became a family of seven in the following years as Jimmy and I brought five sons into this world.

This picture is on the cover of my book *Grossly Outnumbered*! It was taken when Jimmy was running for City Counselman of Sierra Madre.

He did win the election.

John, Jim

Tom, Jac, Tony

Jac   Ginny   Tony.   John   Tom   Jim

Typing this book using Word on my computer, the program wants to correct what it thinks are my mistakes. It is constantly trying to put commas in that I don't and my family and friends don't. Even in this last sentence, it wants a comma after "don't.

Also, it doesn't like using the word "actually". That word must be a Nickoloff family habit because reading our letters, we all use it a lot. Word doesn't even like the way we spell Nickoloff and wants to correct it to two or three other ways.

Another habit we Nickoloffs have is using the word really. It is really fun, really nice, really happy and real big are also no no's in Word. Another criticism is our saying "have to" instead of "must". Is this just a Nickoloff family thing or do other people say, 'I have to do something instead of "I must do something." I consider Word's suggestions, but I do it my way!

Chapter Four

The boys' letters were no less endearing than my husband's. Number One Son Jim's first letter was an apology to me for not practicing the piano.

> February 10, 1959
>
> Dear Mother,
> I have written this note to you to tell you how sorry I am for that incident about practicing the piano. I am very very ashamed!! I hope to try much harder tomorrow!!!!!
>
> Your loving son,
> James Bernard Nickoloff
>
> P.S. I am sorry!

(My mom's address.)
1809 W. 49th Street
L.A. California

> May 16, 1959
>
> Dear Mom and Dad,
> How are you and Hawaii? We are fine. I just got here at Grandma Lola's. Last night, instead of taking John and I here, Grandma Mimi took us to a fish place for dinner. Then we went to Grandma Mimi's and stayed overnight.

Next morning we had a huge breakfast of pancakes, juice, and 1/2 grapefruit, 1 egg, milk and two sausages. When Grandma got dressed we went downtown and saw a mina bird. He said everything I said. If I said "Hi", he said "Hi". He was real funny. After a while we left and went to Robinson's. Grandma did some shopping and I did lots of walking. And looking at jewelry we went to Don Taco's. Taco's made our lunch and Original Barbecue for dessert.

Upon arriving at 1809 West 49th Street, I wrote this letter and am asking you to send me one in return, not quite so boring!! I am very anxious to hear from you Hawaiian tourists. I can guess what you are doing—resting, eating, bathing, sleeping. How could you when your reading this miserable letter!

Love, Jim

P.S. I miss you.

In May of 1963, my in-laws were taking a vacation to Mexico ending up in New York City. It was common in those days to go to the airport to see people off. My father-in-law had a little champaign party at the airport for friends and his travel agent. I guess he was feeling pretty good, as he told the travel agent to make reservations for Jimmy and me and his son Tom and wife Betty to join them when they reached New York City.

My dad came to Sierra Madre and baby-sat my boys except little Tony who stayed with my mom in Los Angeles. Just so you know, I always called my husband Jimmy, so our son was Jim.

Staying on the 48th floor of the Americana Hotel, we were thrilled as the tallest building in Los Angeles was the 25-story City Hall.

We received the following letter from son Jim who was 15 years old at the time:

May 15, 1963

8:30 pm

Dear Mom and Dad,

Well, I finally got around to writing you (which I meant to do twice during this week.) Please excuse the hastiness with which this is written as I'm sure you'll understand the "time" problems (ha) and I'm not exactly in the proper "letter-writing mood" which I'll shortly explain.

Everything went according to plan after you left —until today that is. We all left for school, and when the 9:00 school bell rang, I thought to myself: "There they go!" (And I guess you did from the sound of the first card we received yesterday. We got the 2nd one today). Anyway at 4:30 I got home, and Grandpa Tanny was sitting reading the paper. I've gotten to swimming OK every day so that end of it is all right. Well, anyway, yesterday Tom forgot to come home in time for his piano lesson, but he did get there at 5:15 (5 minutes late) and had an extra long one).

 Then today – Wow! What a day!!!!! In the first place today was the 4th Quarterly English Essentials Test, and I finally finished my geometry final—second in the class, so I got an "A" on it. I went to swimming as usual and John to baseball and Tom to baseball. But Jac! Ah, little Jac! No one knew where he went. Apparently, he went to recreation after school, but from then on no one knew anything.

 When John got home from baseball practice at 6:10 he said that he hadn't seen Jac at all— anywhere up there. And Tom hadn't seen him either past about 3:30. So Grandpa and I started looking—at 6:15. First we went up to Tom's game, but Tom was on the field, so we had to wait until he got in. No, he didn't know where Jac was. Jac hadn't come up to Sierra Madre School. (By the way the Stars lost, but Tom got 1 for 3).

Grandpa and I then checked a few houses around here at 6:30. Having no luck, we drove up to Sierra Mesa School and I checked the playground—Nothing! No one!

By this time, we were furious, so we stormed home and ate—poor John—I'm afraid we weren't too fair with the meal. (John was only fifteen years old and liked to cook and bake cakes.)

At 7:15, still not hearing from Jac (I figured the neighbors would have sent him home by now) I decided to start out again. Debbie Padget said she'd seen him at Heasley Field, so we drove up. Again nothing. Now I was getting a little worried! At 7:30 we (meaning Grandpa, Bob Poolman and several boys up the street, and John on bike) started combing the block—every single likely house.

By 7:45 I was upset and we talked to Tom and Betty Brown. They suggested calling Miss Newton (the principal) or Mr. Marx and seeing if they knew where he'd gone after school. I was just looking up the number when John came bursting in with news of Jac. He was down on Holdman, walking home!

When he got home, he explained! We found out he'd been up at Sierra Mesa School—never left it—behind some classrooms catching frogs in the ivy! Gad's, I was so glad to see the little guy—but at the same time so furious, that I threw him in the tub and sent him to bed. At 8:45 he was still crying—we never touched him, Dad—but he obviously wouldn't go to sleep, so I fed him and made him promise he'd learned his lesson!!!!! Well, so much for that! Tomorrow, I doubt if it'll happen—both Tom and Jac know **EXACTLY** what to do!

Except for this "minor" mishap, everything is A-OK (as they say down at the Cape.). Speaking of this, I suppose you all saw the launch today; I missed it by 2 minutes 45 seconds. If it had been yesterday, I'd have seen it. Pretty neat, huh??!!! I hope it goes 22 orbits! (Jim is writing about Gordon Cooper's U.S. Mercury space flight that did orbit 22 times.)

Well, I guess I'd better go—it's 9:30—I sacrificed the "Beverly Hillbillies". Please keep sending cards—we love 'em. (Boy 48 stories is high, especially thinking back to the measly 25 story L.A. City Hall!)

Say "hi" to all! Have a ball!
Love, Jim, John, Tom + Jac

Jim's letter the next night:

May 16, 1963

Dear Mom and Dad:

It's about 8:00 now, and I just finished helping the little boys with their letters which are enclosed. Jac wasn't too upset at missing you on the phone, but he did want to write a letter to you.

We were surprised to get the call; it was lucky you didn't call a few minutes earlier as Gramps and I had just gotten home from swimming (Jim swam every day all year round). Boy, wasn't the connection good! It sure was hard to believe you were almost 3000 miles away! I could surely tell whose got the money there— Daddy kept saying "Hang up, hang up" and Grampa Jim said he didn't care what it cost, just let him talk!

Our meals have been about as good as you can expect from a 2-month-old cook—actually he's done a good job---we're not starving at least which we probably would be if I had to cook or Grandpa had to. But to be honest, we are looking forward to Sunday night and when you, Mom, get home.

Just a little something I've learned: Mom, I don't really see how you do it—masterminding the activities around here. Most of my time is spent ordering people around-it makes me feel like a grouch, but someone has to tell them to do every little thing. One triumph we've had: Jac finally made his bed—and by himself. Not that I didn't have to ask or rather order him to do it a dozen times 'cause I did. But he did do it which I've been trying to get him to do this whole week.

Well, as I look at the clock it says 8:45 so I gotta go back to the books—I'm still struggling with that darn ninth grade graduation speech. I have gotten some ideas though, and I should be able to turn up with something. This is probably the last letter I'll write so until Sunday--

Bye bye,

Jim, John, Tom, and Jac

P.S. We do miss little Tony, but to be honest it's really a lot easier this way—we've hardly had one fight!

I had to include this letter because it illustrates the fact that Moms are the glue that holds a family together and it made it all worthwhile that I was appreciated.

Jim saved the next letter he received from his Uncle Tom (my brother-in-law) who was an All-American football player from U.S.C. and a lawyer practicing in San Diego dated January 16, 1964.

Dear Jim,

This is to inform you that the shoe is now on the other foot. The other day while I was in trial the opposing counsel asked me if I was related to the fabulous swimmer from Sierra Madre, and I quickly admitted I was.

Congratulations and keep up the good work.

Your proud uncle,
(Signed) Tom

Jim sent me a Mother's Day card in 1991:

Mom (mom), n: 1. familiar form of "mother"

It is derived from the ancient Sanskrit word momm, which means "repairer of torn garments," "healer of small wounds," "finder of lost possessions," and "restaurant."

Jim was the first son to leave home as he had a scholarship to Stanford University. Over the next few years, we received Jim's letters from France, Poland, Finland, Ukraine, Russia, Korea, Jamaica, Mexico, Bolivia and Peru.

When he was twelve, he was watching television when Khrushchev banged his shoe on the table at a United Nations meeting. Jim came out to the kitchen and said to me: "I want to know what he said and not what they said he said."

Pasadena High School was teaching about six languages including Russian, so Jim took both Russian and French and continued with both languages at Stanford.

Stanford offered French students a chance to go to Stanford in Tours, France. The Binot family befriended Jim and invited him and a girl student to come every Wednesday night for dinner as they wanted to practice their English.

Later my husband and I visited the Binots in Tours, and they came to California and visited us. During the Atlanta Olympics, their son Patrick and his son came to Georgia and stayed with us while attending the games.

Following is the first letter we received from France (1968) *le 30 septembre*

Bonjour to you all!

I am sorry that I have not written before now, but we have been on a merry-go-round since we arrived! There are a thousand and one things for me to relate about only 4 days in France-that is why I must write a microscopically—the price of mail goes up dramatically if you exceed a certain limit.

To begin at the beginning: the trip here was very long and tiring, but fun. My body is still not on the correct time—I wake up at 4 a.m. and am exhausted around 5 p.m. But they say it takes a week, so I'll see. We had a beautiful flight to New York, clear all the way. But it was cloudy over the east coast so I didn't get to see much of the city. I was most impressed with the beautiful TWA building!

We left New York at 6:15 and I witnessed a spectacular sunset through the clouds—it was fun thinking it was only 4:30 in California as the darkness descended on everything. Naturally, I saw nothing of the Atlantic—instead we watched our second Doris Day movie of the day (ugh!). The first from S.F. to N.Y. It was so strange to see the sun rising again only six hours later as we approached Paris.

And what a magnificent approach! I can't imagine anything more beautiful than circling the City of Light at dawn. I can never forget that feeling of looking down and seeing homes, fields, and few cars, an entire sleeping city and knowing it was France! We landed at 7 a.m. just as everything came alive—including ourselves after the 15-hour journey. We were met by a marvelous French lady, a member of our staff. I nearly lost my umbrella as we were going through the passport office—I laid it down and forgot it. Just as the bus was getting ready to go, I remembered, ran back and was suddenly faced with having to tell the man my problem—in French! It was a weird feeling—he wanted me to describe it—I guess I didn't look trustworthy or something. So, I said "grand et noire (black)" and I guess that was enough. Orly Airport is very new and modernistic—I like it better than New York or L. A.

The drive to Tours was a struggle—between my mind that wanted to take in everything—and my body which was about ready to crash. I think it was a draw as I saw a great deal and also dozed some. Unfortunately, I was awake enough to notice the atrocious driving habits of the French.

They must certainly be the worst and most unmannered drivers in the world. The bus driver, (being in the largest vehicle) managed to out-maneuver everyone (all tiny, tiny cars). The drive was lovely—the countryside between Paris and Tours is a great deal like region around Portland or Hawaii—very lush. Naturally, I was struck by all the verdure but also by the flowers which are in bloom everywhere. I'm not exaggerating when I tell you that the gas stations along the way were very attractive, because they are all landscaped so nicely. They are very tiny—two pumps and an office—no garage—and they are so numerous. I was a bit surprised to see so many Shell stations—but all very quaint with flowers. I will try to get a picture of one.

  Our arrival in Tours was most welcome (by us!). Exhausted, we ate lunch and collapsed in our rooms. My room is very small—but I won't spend much time in it. The Centre is not luxurious but o.k. I guess. The people who work here are tremendous—so French and such great senses of humor! The city of Tours is very different than I expected—first of all, it is much larger. And second, it is much richer. It is so amazing to walk down the street of a "provincial town" and see block after block of small boutiques that are as nice as anything in Beverly Hills—and nearly as expensive. But the outsides of the buildings are all ancient—and I mean crumbling! But inside they are new and modern. Actually, Tours is distinctly European—exactly what you expect of a European city---but I expected a small town and it's not. The Squares (there are several) all have lovely lawns and flowers and great fountains. C'est magnifique!

    Buying things in Tours is really fun because of the difficulty of the language. At times I feel like a helpless child. I can converse rather well, but if I need something technical, it's quite a challenge trying to describe it in a roundabout way. For instance, we needed an adaptor plug for our wall outlet (for our razors) it took us all afternoon to find one and buy one. But les Tourangeau (the people of Tours) are very willing to listen and try to understand.

    When I arrived, I had a note in my box from Jacqueline Binot, Patrick's mother. I was very happy to see it. They invited me to lunch on Sunday—but it was more like a Scandia dinner! M. Binot is a kick and Mme Binot is very youthful looking. (I'm sure she dyes her hair, too, Mom.). Three of Patrick's 4 sisters and cousin Christine so M. Binot and I were outnumbered.

He laughed when I told him about the ratio at our house. The meal was elegant. We began with wine martinis (which I choked on but said I liked anyway). Then we had salami type meat and bread, then corned beef and cabbage and vegetables with red wine and finally ice cream. I had to leave before the café au lait.

The Binots live in an old old home, almost falling apart on the outside, but splendid inside (about like Grandma Mimi's on Citrus. They live across the river from me overlooking all of Tours.

They have invited me to come to dinner twice a week which will be a welcome change from the food here. (Ugh!). They are wonderful, just like Gene told me. I am anxious to see Patrick when he gets here. I think I did okay with conversing with them—we talked about the same things you and Patrick did at our house.

Sunday afternoon we visited two chateaux about which I already wrote. Today (Monday) we took French tests and had a lecture on the Revolution of May in France by a professor from the Sorbonne.

This weekend we are going to Munich (Germany) for the Oktoberfest—a huge celebration (beer bath). We are going for only $29 on the train round trip—because over 25 are in the party we get 50% off in Germany and 40% off in France.

    A few of us non-drunkards hope to hitchhike to Salzburg (Austria) about 65 miles from Munich. I hate to run off the first weekend I'm in France, but the rate is so good (a onetime offer) and Oktoberfest is a once a year thing, besides I might not get to Germany again. We leave Thursday afternoon—first to Paris, then to Salzburg, then Stuttgart, then Munich. Should be great! Bye for now-please let everyone know what I'm doing so I won't have to write so many letters.

                        Love to all, Jim

le 8 Octobre, 1968

    Having finally received a letter—three in fact—I guess I can begin to write again. I enjoyed both your letters, especially Dad's enclosure—but where are mes "amis"?

    I have a great deal to report this time—so much that I feel almost like waiting until I get home to tell you about it—but I know that you will appreciate even an abbreviated version.

To begin then—le voyage merveilleux a Munich! We left Tours Thursday afternoon and were in Paris at about 7 o'clock. As it was necessary to change train stations to catch the train for Munich, we got to see un peu de Paris also. My first experience on the Metro (subway) was memorable. We got lost, but finally made it to la Gare de l'Est (Eastern Station). We took the Orient Express which goes all the way to Budapest from Paris. European trains are fast, clean, and always on time—because they are electric. We were crowded 8 to a compartment—so it was difficult to sleep. I'd say I got about 5 hours.

When we awoke, we were in Germany and already I could notice changes in the countryside passing by. There seems to be a great deal more modern buildings—mostly built since the war—than in France. But still the predominate scene is one of ages old homes scattered across green, green fields. All so picturesque—exactly as you'd imagine it—except it is real.

Our arrival in Munich heralded a new experience—total lack of ability to communicate verbally—French is hard enough, but none of us spoke any German. The first problem was to find a place to stay and as it was the last week of

Octoberfest (Europe's largest celebration) it was difficult.

Finally, after three hours, two friends and I happened on to a "palace" quite by accident—and for only $2.50 a night. Actually, it was a penthouse apartment belonging to someone. There seems to be a great deal more modern buildings—mostly built since the war—than in France. But still the predominant scene is one of ages-old homes scattered across green, green fields. All is so picturesque—exactly as you'd imagine it—except it's real.

Our arrival in Munich heralded a new experience—total lack of ability to communicate verbally—French is hard enough—but none of us (42 went) spoke any German. The first problem was to find a place to stay, and as it was the last week of Octoberfest (Europe's largest celebration!) it was difficult.

Finally, after 3 hours, two friends and I happened on to a "palace" —quite by accident—and for the wardrobe was complete, we had a kitchen (with some food!), a stereo with a large record collection, and a shower (something I don't have in Tours-only a bath). Besides this, we had an outside patio—with flowers and a spectacular view of the city and only one block from the grounds of Octoberfest!

Friday afternoon, we took a great tour of the city (bus)—saw all the important places like where the Munich agreement was signed, etc. There are so many palaces, platz (squares with great fountains) and museums—I could have used a week there.

Later in the afternoon we met two guys who were more or less sharing the apartment, returnees from the Peace Corps in Nigeria—really great guys—who took us to Octoberfest the first night.

I simply cannot describe the Octoberfest-you could never imagine it! People had raved about it to me—and still I had no conception at all! About the best way to describe it is it's like Disneyland, the Pomona Fair, and New Year's Eve all rolled into one. In 16 days over 5 million people attend--about 500,000 there one night alone (Friday). It's a celebration of the harvest of the hops, so you can imagine how much beer is consumed. The waitresses in the hofbraus (beer houses) carry 10 mugs at a time—I have one so you will see how big they are (1 liter) and heavy. <u>Everyone</u> is having a ball—it's really contagious. I can't remember ever having seen so many completely happy people all at once—bands play drinking songs for hours. I hope my picture turns out. And then there are hundreds of rides, food and candy stalls—it's really gigantic! But, it ends at 10:30—which is really a good thing, I guess, when you consider how much beer has been consumed! It starts around 4 in the afternoon so there is plenty of time to get smashed—but the only drunks you see are Americans. The Germans can hold theirs. All in all, it was a giant party—a time to let yourself go—and we did—and loved every minute of it.

Saturday morning, we walked around the city. It is true that European cities are compact, but it is still a lot of walking. We saw a couple great churches and the city hall with its famous glockenspiel which played at 11 am every day.

After lunch we went by train to Dachau, the concentration camp of 1933-1945 where 32,000 were killed. If ever there could be a complete opposite from Octoberfest! There are not words to describe that hell on earth. I don't think it was morbid curiosity which led me there. After all, it is a fact. Everyone is quiet there—all is still in fact. There is a museum, which amazed me. The Germans are really open about the whole thing, but I noticed that no Germans were taking pictures—only foreigners. All is just like it was during those years except that most of the barracks have been removed with gravestones put in their place. I could describe it in detail to you, but that would serve no purpose. We have all read about such horrors—but there was something about standing there, being there.... It is all summed up in the beautifully simple monument erected only last month. Its only inscription is "Never Again" written in four languages.

    After that. I could go every night for a year it was so much fun! At this one Hofbrau there was this little old German lady (about 60-65) who kept pushing me off my bench (they are back-to-back)—and everyone is crowded together anyway). Finally, I gave her a shove (rump to rump) and she turned around and laughed so hard! She talked on and on to us in German—we tried to explain that we didn't speak any, but she continued, undaunted. We became such good friends that I finally understood her meaning—she was my "Deutsche mama" and I pointed to her husband and said, "Deutsch papa" and she nodded. I have it all on film—so you will see how merry we all were!

    We didn't get to bed until after midnight and were up at 5:30 a.m.—our train left at 7. We all spent the trip reading The Red and the Black (500 pages due on Monday), but I got to see most of the countryside---the leaves are just beginning to turn color which is gorgeous—red, orange, and yellow against green!

 In Stuttgart I really had a scare—a friend and I got off the train for some nourriture (food) and when we got back the train was gone. I had visions of some enormous price to get back to Tours—but the train was just changing tracks. Needless to say, I stayed aboard the rest of the trip…. that is, until Paris where we had to change depots again. Only this time we took the Metro to get something to eat—and missed our train to Tours by 4 minutes—and the next one didn't leave till 11:56 p.m. (this was at 7:30). So, at 2:30 am we finally straggled into the Center—exhausted after the 21-hour trip—but so glad we'd made it nonetheless!

 There is so much else I have to relate—the food I've tried, the "tininess" (smallness) of the French people (I don't think I've seen a man over 5'5"), their different manners—and, of course, all about life at the Centre—which is great! But I must get this off—I've so much to do! I guess you must get the picture anyway—I'm **ECSTATIC!** I think of you all so often and wish you could share this fantastic experience with me!! C'est tout pour le moment—j'ecrirai encore las semaine prochain!

Je vous embrasse, Jim

The following letter had a letterhead:

Hotel Conde Duque
Plaza Conde Valle de Suchil, 5
Madrid-15

November 12—Hello all! I have a great deal to relate this time—I think I'll spread it over a couple post cards and this letter. To begin with, a week ago I met Kenny Hensie (our old neighbor). We spent a nice day together at the Chateau de Blois. He bought me a real good dinner in Tours. I was going to send some pictures back with him, but some people in the group want duplicates of my slides. I think I'll have them all developed here. The ones so far have turned out beautifully (actually I'm ecstatic over them!) and besides, I like to see them!

Last week at the Binots we showed them on the screen—everyone raved. It was quite a project as Patrick and Mr. Binot were not home—just Mme and the girls and unmechanical moi! First, we had the projector backwards. No one could understand why nothing was appearing on the screen until Annette noticed the picture on the fireplace behind us! Then we put the magazine in backwards and after Marie-Noel pushed the button (changer), the whole thing shot out onto the floor! We were in hysterics for 15 minutes!

It was just as well we were laughing so hard because no one (least of all me) was in hysterics over the election that day—which brings me to another news item. The night of the election the regional French television and radio stations wanted to tape the Stanford students awaiting the returns (the coverage was fantastic, by the way—continued and gleaned from all 3 American networks so we had the best/worst of everything).

Anyway, the television wanted to interview a couple students and yours truly made his French T.V. debut—in French, naturally. It was really a kick. I tried to explain how I kinda supported Humphrey as the lessor of 3 evils. The moderator asked several questions and we answered-but I didn't get to see (or hear—most Frenchmen don't have T.V.s—the Binots don't) it on TV because they weren't sure when it would be run! (As for the elections themselves, I guess Nixon's the one (the one what?) great to see Rafferty's defeat (but not ecstatic over Cranston either.)

As you can see from the letterhead—I find myself in Spain, land of the conquistadores, flamenco, and <u>Madrid</u>—what a city! Our train trip from Tours was beautiful. We left at midnight—slept on couchettes (a kind of bed—4 bunks high—but comfortable)—crossed the border about 9 a.m.—had to change trains because Spanish tracks are a different size. The trip through the Pyrenees is unbelievable—I know I say this about every place, but you must make it to Spain.

It rained most of the way but we were treated to the most magnificent cloud formations I've ever seen and several bright rainbows. Spain is very much like California—there are contrasts—but the same. I think we all became a little homesick seeing the beauty of our own California reflected in the Spanish countryside.

One does not wonder long why the Spaniards of old settled in Mexico and California. (You ask, why go to Spain to see California?) It is difficult to explain—but for some reason it's a <u>must!</u> It's so much more interesting having studied Spanish history (the explorers, Columbus, etc.). I know a lot more about Spanish history than French. Seeing places Ferdinand and Isabella built means more than seeing some Louis-or-other's castle. And the Spanish names all recall places at home.

Madrid to me is described in one word—romantic and in the fullest sense of the word.

Maybe because the weather is so beautiful here (it's much warmer than Tours) but it's also because of the people. No people are more outgoing—friendly!

We met some Spaniards (students) in the street last Saturday night and they invited us to go along with them to mesones (café-restaurant) in Old Madrid. It was just fantastic—we grooved till 2:30 singing Spanish songs (we faked it—after a little wine no one knew the difference), dancing the flamenco and drinking vino tinto (red wine) and eating Spanish omelette (called tortilla here). After the mesor closed, we went out into the streets and continued our merry-making. One girl in our group of 6 got sick and one of the Spaniards drove 3 of us back to the hotel and then 2 of us back to the mesor. Pretty nice!

Last night we met them again—again went "mesonesing" heard the most beautiful classical guitarist imaginable! Then went to Piccadilly—local discotheque—and danced till 3:30. Getting up for Toledo this morning was un peu difficult!

The sight of Madrid and surrounding area are also spectacular. The Prado Museum (filled with Goya, El Greco, Rubens, etc.) is the best in the world—better than the Louvre, according to all critics. We saw a church cut into a granite mountain that was the most spectacular man-made thing I've seen in Europe. And Toledo was grand. We visited El Greco's home—lots of his originals are there. Well, I must close—will continue on cards I want to collect. By for now.

Adios, mio amor—Jim

While Jim was attending Stanford in France, the students did a tour of Europe including Russia. We received the following letter from Poland dated December 21, 1968:

Snow everywhere. The air is like the coldest night air in California. All day. All night. A city of night. Dark at midmorning. Dark in mid-afternoon. At high noon there are low grey clouds which obscure all light. Dark grey buildings, warm pink people. Rows and rows of drab apartment houses, but big open spaces everywhere. Nowhere is there any green, or blue of the sky. Or yellow of the sun. Just white everywhere. But this is Warsaw.

"Ten minutes to the Russian border."

"Just think, the Iron Curtain." The snowfall in Vienna had made the cold worth it. But Prague is ahead. Prague! Invaded city! What will we find?

Look at the countryside. Just like a picture post card of New England. We will have a white Christmas.

"Dpabenibyume! (Hello) Are you in the Czeck army?"

"Yes, I am."

"Would you mind speaking in Russian?"

"I would rather not."

But he wanted to communicate. As do all Czechs...with all Americans.

In a beer hall about fifteen middle-aged Czechs gather around a group of American students. "We in America do not understand why the Russians came."

"We in Prague do not understand why they stay." The conversation continued on into the night with the twenty-one-year-old Czech soldier.

Russian was better than silence. "What are you doing now in the way of lessening the Russian grip? "Nothing can be done."

The sightseeing tours of Europe—very good, very interesting, but about the same. More monuments, more palaces, more kings, more people in each European capitol, too, but here they are different. There is only one thing on their minds, one thing only. Freedom. Freedom from Russia. They do not hide their constant thought. On a building: "Viva Dubcek." On a bus window written in the frost "Russians go home." A young Czech said, "The greatest sight I ever saw was a Russian tank burning the first day of the invasion."

"What can be done?" The same answer: "Nothing." There are soldiers everywhere, military trucks everywhere. Prague is a military base. Looks just like a World War 11 movie.

Warsaw was destroyed 85%. And 50% of its population destroyed. Mostly after German defeat was certain. But destroyed by retreating Germans. Of course, it is today a modern city. Virtually everything has been built in my lifetime. Still, it remains plain. When you have no money for food, you do not waste it on beautiful architecture. "Communism was the only answer for Poland's economic recovery. We did not have American money as did Germany and Japan to start the investments rolling."

Kiev, Ukraine. 6:15 pm   January 1, 1969
Happy New Year!

I just have a few minutes before dinner to dash off this letter. My hands are frozen so it's a little difficult to write—but I do want to describe the most unusual New Year's I've spent yet.

Leningrad was magnificent—certainly one of the most beautiful cities in the world. The Neva River divides in the city and there were canals wandering everywhere—mostly frozen. And instead of drab grey and black buildings, it is filled with pastel yellow, green and pink ones.

Having studied so much about Saint Peters-burg and Leningrad, I found it extremely interesting---it was built by Peter the Great and was the capital of the Russian Empire until 1917. It was also the cradle of the Revolution. On Monday evening some of us went to the house where Lenin planned the final details of the Revolution. It is now a little museum of his plans. We met with about six old Bolsheviks—men who were only about 20 when they took part in the up-rising. We had a question and answer session for about 2 hours ranging from our lives in America to Czechoslovakia. It was great being in the very room where Lenin and his compatriots drew up the plans, talking with actual participants.

Tuesday morning we were scheduled to leave by plane for Kiev. The night before we had had a huge bash as a good-by to Leningrad—so naturally we were anxious to get on the 10:30 a.m.

plane and sleep. However, it turned into that Lincoln-Nebraska flight all over again.

They kept telling us that the weather in Kiev was bad but that it could change at any time and the plane would go. Finally, at 3 in the afternoon some of us went back into the city for a while. We had dinner at 8 and started getting ready to greet the new year in the Leningrad Airport (without anything to drink). About 10 p.m. one of our Russian guides and I went to get a record player—the temperature was close to 0°--the coldest in my life.

We were returning with the record player about 10:30 when I jokingly said: "Wouldn't it be funny if we missed the plane?" Well, I wasn't far from wrong: everyone was just getting ready to board. But, the thing was there are only two planes a day from Leningrad to Kiev, and neither one had gone the day before. Consequently, there were quite a few people anxious to get on our plane.

I don't know if they don't reserve places or what, but we were told that a bus was to take us out to the plane so that we would be ahead of the crowd that was about to mob the plane. Well, our driver couldn't find the plane at first—when we finally found it, the crowd was already at the bottom of the boarding ramp.

Now, the most amazing thing I have ever witnessed took place. Our guides (two girls) and our Italian guide pushed to the front of the crowd and managed to hold them back while a number of us pushed through. In the struggle, I dropped everything, including my boarding ticket which I couldn't find. I was just freezing there on the windy and snowy runway.

After a few minutes, we at the back of the crowd couldn't push through—so we started handing all of our junk to those who had made it and began climbing up over the sides of the ramp. I was lucky to make it—because the Russians were naturally indignant and tried to prevent us from climbing up. But our guide kept yelling to come on—so we pushed each other up the eight-foot icy side and onto the stairway—and collapsed inside in our seats! It was really an experience—I'm not kidding when I say we had to battle our way on board!

We left at 11 p.m. on a prop plane that was the noisiest thing I've ever heard. Exhausted as we were, I couldn't sleep it was so noisy and besides we had to greet the New Year! At midnight we had a countdown. We had all made New Year's hats out of our free copies of Pravda given to each passenger and someone had brought confetti, so we made a shambles of the plane. But, what a New Years—high in the skies over snowy Mother Russia. I doubt I will ever top that!!!

We arrived in a snowfall in Kiev—which is warmer than Leningrad, but snowier. When we got to our hotel at 2:30 a.m. there was a party in full swing—a group of Yugoslavs. We feasted (and I do mean feasted) and danced and drank until 5:30, then finally collapsed in bed. I tasted my first caviar (not too fond of it) and had enough cognac to last me for a long while.

We got up at one in the afternoon (2 a.m. in California)—I suppose you were in the middle of it out there. We had a tour of Kiev overlooking the Dnieper River so famous in Russian literature. Everyone in Kiev was out promenading today— everyone! It was really great, and the new fallen snow was so beautiful. All of us from California raved and raved!

Unfortunately, we leave tonight at 3 in the morning on the 19-hour train ride to Budapest. Sure wish we had another day in Kiev—but we're having another party tonight—no point in going to bed till 3! Sure hope your New Year's was happy!

Love always, Jim

January 8, 1969

Happy New Year!

And now for the real truth about my trip to Eastern Europe and Russia. I don't know if you could tell from the cards I sent, but I didn't really say a great deal—except, perhaps, in the letter from Warsaw. But there was a reason, as I shall explain.

Crossing the Iron Curtain (a term all Eastern Europeans, and Russians as well, are aware of) was something I had expected to be very dramatic. Instead, the Czech border was exactly like any other in Europe—no customs, just a simple passport check and the usual "extra simplicity" for Americans. Furthermore, as I described in my first card from Prague, I made the acquaintance of a young Czech soldier quite easily and conversed for a couple hours with him in broken Russian. This was my first contact with the openness of the Czechs---a soldier was willing to discuss the events of August! We always approached the Czechs with care—but never did we encounter anyone who was afraid to speak with us about anything. I regretted having always to communicate in Russian, but the people were so anxious to talk with us. I was surprised at their knowledge of American politics—much better than the French. I found out that they do listen to Radio Free Europe and the Voice of America.

The other thing we encountered for the first time in Prague was the black market. Our Italian guide as well as our two Czech guides (two students) told us about it as soon as we arrived. It was never really encouraged that we deal on the black market, but we realized that it was easily accessible and not at all strictly controlled. In fact, our Czech guides were willing to change our money for 3 times the official rate. The reason that the black market is so big is that in every socialist country there are certain stores that are geared to tourists and which usually have the very best merchandise available in the country-and it is sold only for foreign currency. In addition, for people going to other countries from a socialist one, it is better to smuggle foreign currency out since the governments permit very little to go out legally and give very bad exchange rates at the border. Thus, we soon saw just how big the black market was in Prague and in Warsaw.

There were always people waiting around in hotel lobbies who would approach you and say "change money?" followed by their personal exchange rate. Well, I'm not exaggerating when I say that everyone in our group changed his money on the black market, mostly for 4 and 5 times the official rate.

As you can imagine, this gave us a tremendous buying power ($2 changed gave one $10 buying power)—but we soon learned another side to the story—there is virtually nothing worth buying in most of the countries. The stores were extremely barren; of course, it was just a few days till Christmas and perhaps, there had been more—but still the difference between Vienna and Prague was striking. One thing we did notice was that there were bookstores everywhere—nearly one per block in Prague and Warsaw. And people on buses, etc. read books instead of newspapers.

Helsinki. June 27, 1970

Hi Folks!

Helsinki! What a great way to begin a second voyage through the wonderland that is Europe! New York was really exciting for me—in many ways, I felt like a foreigner in that city—but now that I'm really a "stranger" (my Finish vocabulary consists of two words—thanks and "sale" everything's on sale here!) I know what it's like all over again. Some of the thrill is missing—but the charm is still here. I think I'm much more perceptive now, perhaps, because I'm not so starry-eyed about it all. Nevertheless, it's hard not to be overwhelmed with the beauty of Finland and especially her capital.

We're living in a student hotel--dormitory outside the city—but inside or out, Helsinki is not really a city anyway. It consists of hundreds of islands separated by large "lakes" (one or two miles wide) which are really connected to the sea. The downtown section is very small—you can walk from one end to the other—but the "city" extends for miles along the islanded (a word?) coast. But the clincher is the forest which seems to push the city right into the Baltic Sea—all of Finland appears as a forest from the air broken here and there by small farms--and, of course, here by the city of Helsinki.

In many ways Helsinki reminds me of Leningrad or what I picture Leningrad in the summer to be: pastel buildings, which left their impression on me forever in the great Russian metropolis are also very common here. I still can't understand why the European cities have not adopted this beautiful technique. The quay at the harbor in Helsinki is lined with a blue, a pink and a yellow and a white building. A block away is an orange one.

Helsinki is filled with its Russian past. Finland did not win independence until 1917. The Russian church is entirely made of brick! I wanted to see the inside so this afternoon I wandered in and began to look around. All of a sudden I heard a choir begin to sing and then a wedding procession marched in. I happened to be near the altar so there was no escape—and (catch this) I was wearing my jeans and sandals and a crumby t-shirt! Everyone else was dressed formally! Embarrassed? You bet—anyway I was glad to see the wedding ceremony—even from the altar in full view of everyone!

I still have not related to you the most fantastic feature of this city. I'll probably be raving about this the rest of my life, but really you just can't believe the white nights!

The first night we were here I went to bed at 9:30 'cause I was literally exhausted. When I woke up it was light—looked like about 7:00 or 7:30 does at home. I felt terrible but I assumed that I was still tired from the last two weeks in general. However, when I looked at the clock, it said 2:30! Naturally I didn't believe it, so I started to get up. One of my roommates woke up too and he insisted that the clock had to be right—so we checked his watch—and sure enough, it was

2:30 a.m.! I was still unconvinced—it was like day but I went back to bed anyway. At 8 I woke up again.

Last night I went with a couple other kids to this island-fortress off the coast a ways to watch the sunset. It finally went below the horizon at 10:30 but not very far. At 11:30 the whole sky was still light though the eastern part was very pink (sunset or sunrise?).

At midnight, (we were still on the island) the southern part was a little dark, but you still couldn't see a single star anywhere in the sky because of the light (how did the Norsemen become such good sailors, I wonder!)

And, of course, no matter where you are, it always begins to get lighter after midnight because noon is always the time the sun is highest in the sky—so at 1:30 sunrise occurs, that is the sun comes up over the horizon and for the next 21 hours, it is day!!! There is never a minute that you can't see well enough to read the newspaper. Of course, winters are just the opposite which is the price that must be paid for this spectacular sunrise show!

We leave for Leningrad tomorrow—an 11-hour train ride. It's only 8 hours the other direction which means the 3-hour difference is made in customs at the Soviet border (the Finns don't look at a thing!). I hope the weather there is as nice as here—it was about 80 degrees when we landed in Helsinki---I couldn't believe it could get that warm this far north (but with 21 hours of sunshine what can you expect!)

The Russian program sounds very vigorous—but then all we've had is orientation discussions, so I really don't know yet. I still haven't recovered from the time change and the long flight (it was 9 hours from New York to Amsterdam and then 2 hours to Helsinki).

We stopped in Amsterdam for refueling and I was able to call the Binots for $1.50 and explain that I've given their address as my forwarding address. Mrs. Binot thought my call was a joke at first, she was so surprised! When we got to Helsinki, we had to wait an hour for our luggage to be unloaded because the Shah of Iran had just arrived, and he had to be taken care of first!

Until whenever, Jim

The summer following Jim's graduation from Stanford, he received a scholarship to Leningrad University with another opportunity to practice his Russian. This was 1970 and Russia was having a severe drought and about the only food available was potatoes.

During the Cold War the U.S.A. and Russia had dual track and field meets from 1958 to 1985 in Leningrad. Ted Turner started the Goodwill Games after that.

When Jim and his friend tried to get tickets to these games in 1970, they were told it was sold out. They walked to the stadium and saw the U.S. team arriving. They joined them and they gave them stuff to carry like they were part of the team. Inside there were plenty of empty seats. Jim said that when they saw our team marching down the field carrying the American Flag, it was very emotional for them.

Leningrad, August 3, 1970

Hello, hello!

This morning we returned from Tallinn which is the capitol of Estonia. Yes, that's right—who ever goes to Estonia?! That's what we thought until we went—but it turned out to be a great surprise. First of all, it has the highest standard of living in the Soviet Union—the difference between it and Leningrad is marked—this meant for us <u>good food</u>—something we never get here.

We were there only one day but it was perfect weather. I spent most of the afternoon (after the normal boring tour in the a.m.) on the beach—the water (Baltic Sea) was like a bathtub and very shallow (3 feet) for about a mile out! I even got sun-burned; it was so hot. All in all, it was hard to believe we were still in the Soviet Union—the city is a German town built in 1200-1400—very beautiful—and thin people (something not to be found in Leningrad).

This afternoon we have classes from 3 to 7—if that isn't too much! I've missed a few times (last week—due to some horrible stomach flu –5 days)—so I guess I'd better show up—really don't want to as there's so much left to do in Leningrad and we leave next Sunday!

Most of my Russian friends have left for the south (Yalta or other places around the Black Sea) for a month and a half –so it's really not as much fun here as it was till last week. I've kinda opted for people over classes and class work—consequently, I'm sometimes in a little trouble (I've spent several nights away from the dorm) Russian parties last late—and we're not supposed to ever do that! In addition we're supposed to stay within 40 km of Leningrad at all times—but I've disregarded this one too as there's too much to see beyond the limit. I'm really not at all anxious to leave—Moscow does not thrill me at all.

Well, I suppose I'd better wish Mom and Jac "Happy Birthdays" with this mail service, there's no telling when you'll get this—also congratulations to Bob—I would have sent a telegram but it's $4.00 for 8 words (minimum). Hope all is well with you—I think I've received all your mail—one day last week I got 5 letters—one mailed from France took 21 days while yours took "only" 16. And please don't forget to send me the money order in France—I'm down to $45 right now! Bye for now and thanks for the mail,
Me

The Vietnam War was in progress. Son John received the number 256 in the draft (relief) and Jim received number 25 (panic). He knew he would be drafted when he graduated, so he had applied for conscientious objector status and applied for the Peace Corps. I forwarded an application from the Peace Corps for Jim to teach English in South Korea, a third world country at that time. From the land of potatoes, Jim arrived in the land of rice! Rice every day for the next three years!

Seoul, Korea.   Feb. 15, 1971

HELLO*O*O*O* CALIFORNIA! Are you still there?

It was, of course, a bit of a surprise to be sitting in a tiny Korean village in the middle of nowhere, listening to the news on a radio and to suddenly learn that my home city had been shaken to the ground. News reports being somewhat sketchy here, I have been unable to find out how much, except that the San Fernando Valley seemed to bare the brunt of the shock. (Newspapers here are commonly printed in Chinese so even if my Korean were very good, I would have been unable to read the news.). I trust I will receive a report in your next letter.

I arrived in Seoul last Friday after a week in the country—and was pleased to receive two letters from you. I am sorry that I did not include this information in my earlier notes, but I guess in my excitement (and illness--I did have mononucleosis, by the way) I forgot to mention it: Yes, I did buy a Pentax camera in Tokyo for $91.00 I am told they will sell for about $170 at home. I have not yet finished a roll of film, so I don't know what the slides are like yet. The first roll will probably be a bust anyway as I am just beginning to understand the camera (you are aware of my mechanical gifts) but it is fun and I'm beginning to learn); you can't let an expensive piece of equipment like that sit around!

My week in the country was very enjoyable as I was finally feeling well. That seems to make a difference—Korea can look so different from one day to the next. The town I was in was really "country" - i.e., it was a one bath house town and has no bakeries. (Two indications of the size of a town in Korea). It was the capital of Packcho's Dynasty about 1,000 years ago—and is located in a beautiful part of the country. Although rather isolated, three hours from Chouju and two hours from Taegu by dirt road. The buses on those roads are really something—everybody and everything rides them as there is no other way to get around. A goat in a white cotton bag traveled next to me.

Although we were supposed to be practice teaching, the best part of the week was spent outside of that (freezing) school. One day we climbed the mountain which rises directly behind the village. Packcho ruins cover the mountains. On top, under deep snow, is a beautiful pagoda-like look-out tower. From there you can see the whole valley, and in all directions extend brown rice fields.

We slipped and slid down the back of the mountain and suddenly rounding a huge rock, we could see a tiny Buddhist temple about the size of our house, brilliantly painted in orange, blue, red and green and yellow. It's built into the mountain rock, almost as if it is cowering from the stormy blasts of winter which whip up the mountain side. Like a tiny Christmas tree ornament, it hangs from the pine-covered mountain high above the rice paddies below.

We entered the big green doors and beheld three golden Buddhas, sitting stiffly among the treasures of the temple. The stillness was broken only by the chattering of the monks next door in their quarters, I presume—and the howling wind outside. The peaceful beauty of the place convinced me there is a Calm in the land and inspiration too.

(My note: Korea is known as the Land of the Morning Calm).

The next day we were invited to a sixty-first birthday, called wan gup in Korean, the father of one of the teachers in our school. It's the most important birthday in a person's life in Chinese culture, because the cycle of life is thought to be sixty (or five twelves) so when a person lives beyond his allotted sixty, it is quite an event.

The celebration took place way out in the country at the old man's home. From Pujo, which

I said was practically nothing more than a wide spot in the road, we had to travel another hour by bus (This road was unbelievable, I swear) to a tiny village of maybe 100 people—all African grass roof style. But we weren't there yet. A man in traditional Korean clothing—really everyone in the village wore traditional clothes—led us across the rice paddies for about two and one-half miles up into a mountain canyon.

There perched on a narrow shoulder of land was a compound of about five houses. No electricity, no conveniences. And when we arrived, there were about fifty to sixty people there, gaily dressed and obviously very surprised to see us (two Americans). We immediately became the center of attention and along with the other teachers from our school were shown to one of the "huts' where I ate "strange and wondrous" things for the next three hours and washed it down with makholli, Koreans most famous alcoholic drink.

The Korean custom of drinking is worth relating: When a person has finished his glass or cup of makholli, he offers it to the other person, fills it for him and then the other person is expected to divide it. This is always done very ceremoniously with the two-hand polite exchange as I showed you—at first it is ceremoniously. Gradually, as you might expect the ceremony breaks down as the alcohol begins to go to work.

We emerged from the bungalow spent and it was only with great effort and several rest stops along the way (Koreans go to the bathroom anywhere) that I was able to navigate the narrow paths and foot bridge back across the rice paddies.

But that was only the beginning having missed one bus, we retired to a makholli house where we drank for another hour and a half till the bus came. Having left for the party at two (school was cancelled so the teachers could go) we arrived home at the respectable hour of 7:30 in a most unrespectable state. Not me, of course, my state hardly mattered-but the vice-principal! You should have seen him.

We left Pujo on Friday—after our farewell speech to the faculty (three sentences in Korean) and arrived in Seoul that afternoon. But this time Seoul had changed! Never have I been so forcefully struck with the importance of relativity!

Compared to the two weeks spent in Choyju and Pujo, the capital did, indeed, appear to be a completely modern city. Just seeing people dressed in the latest and not staring at us—excited me. Last night I went to see "Anna of the Thousand Days" and felt just like I was in New York again!

  Yesterday was an unusual day—I feel like I am just running at the mouth (pen)—but this experience will certainly be one I will place among the "Ten Weirdest Places I Have Been". We (all of us) boarded a bus and headed due north of Seoul and within two hours we had arrived at the site of one of the most incomprehensible--and absurd human enterprises on the face of the earth: Pan Mun Jon and the Joint Security Council Area, site of the "talks" between the U.N. Command (U.S.) and the North Koreans (always written North here).

  Having signed a paper stating my full knowledge that I was entering a combat zone—we crawled through the D.M.Z. by-passing a site where ambushes have recently taken place and being preceded and followed by machine gun carrying truck escort.

  At the site of the negotiations, we were less than 100 feet from the North Korean guard—and inside the building we actually walked across the line into North Korea by walking around the table. There is a picture of the place in the National Geographic as I recall. If you think arguing about the shape of the table at the Paris

Peace conference was outrageous, you should hear what they discuss here. Man has certainly found ways to manifest his stupidity—or weakness-but I won't go into all that. Much too depressing.

And so, in a nutshell—that's the story of the last week. Certainly, more enjoyable than the last three.

I think we will be leaving for our permanent sites on Thursday or Friday.

Andong, Korea, Feb. 20, 1971

Hello again!

I have several things to announce. First on February 16, it becomes official—not your marriage (heavens after all these years—and babies) but I was finally sworn in as a Peace Corp Volunteer, having at last graduated from my four-month status as a Trainee, and hereby entering the employ of the Big Bad Government in a capacity I think I will find acceptable. I can't say that any of us (we now number thirty-one) one guy married one of our Korean language instructors the day after we arrived in Korea) was unhappy to see the end of the training. We had completed—no make that endured exactly four months. We were all champing at the bit to get out of Seoul and out of training and down to business.

So here I am. As you will note above, I am writing this letter in Andong, which is my new home for a while, I hope. We received our site placements on Tuesday, met our co-teachers (Korean) and the principals of our schools on Thursday, and on Friday, on my birthday, I was on the train to Andong—separated at last from the "group" and not believing that the culmination of all those months of language, culture, English teaching, and other assorted—in short the end of the training and the Real Beginning (of what we all asked ourselves) had suddenly arrived.

Andong is located on the Kyong sang puk do (province) about due north from the city of Taegu. If you draw a pencil between Pusan and Seoul, Andong is a little to the right. I think I am about 3 hours from Taegu by train, maybe 2 ½ hours by bus, and it took six hours by train from Seoul. The beaches on the eastern coast (supposedly very beautiful) are at least four hours away. I am pretty much in the middle of nowhere.

It is of course too soon to write any meaningful words about Andong—I've only been here one day. All I know for sure is that my co-teachers cannot speak a word of English, and consequently I'm kind of in the dark about everything. I've moved into a house—sort of a boarding house I think—but as I say, I am not sure about it. i.e. I don't know yet how much I'll be paying, etc. This afternoon we walked over to the school, and last night I wandered around town—it's quite small.

(My note: It looked and seemed very small but really had 80,000 residents.)

Monday, I'll go to school and meet the teachers—which means I'll have to give a little speech in Korean.

I had a haircut today. My first here. Shave, hair wash the whole thing for fifty cents. I think I'll be keeping my hair real short here judging by the teachers. Love, Jim

One very interesting letter to my husband from Jim arrived from Korea on Ground Hog's Day. Significant because his Dad was born on Ground Hog's Day in 1924 and this was my husband's 48th birthday. Four twelves. Jim's letter:

"The year 1972 is the Year of the Rat in the Chinese (and Korean) calendar, the first of the 12-year cycle.

"The rat was chosen to be first among the animals who represent the 12 years for this reason: When he was dying, the Great Buddha called all the animals to his bedside. The cow started out first, faithful as always, but the rat, clever animal that he is, jumped on the cow's back and rode all the way. At the last minute, the rat jumped down and arrived first at the Buddha's bedside, thus becoming the first of the 12 animals who came---is the year in which you (the eldest son, a very important position to occupy in this part of the world) are 4 twelves in age, and I, your eldest son, am exactly half that, being 2 twelves in age. (It is also interesting for Chinese fortune tellers or whoever, that both of our mothers are also older than we by 2 twelves this year.) ---is the year in which I send you birthday wishes after 12 moons in Asia (and that alone is pretty weird!)"

I have been fascinated with Oriental culture since I was a little girl in Long Beach shopping on the Pike in the Japanese stores for little carved animals. And later I became intrigued with netsukes, the twelve little animals from the Buddhist calendar carved out of ivory or jade. My collection has many rats because I was also born in the year of the rat. One my cousin Jean gave me is by my front door. She was the Year of the Ox.

Andong, Feb. 26th, 1971

Dear Family,

A week in Andong and Korea is beginning to come alive for me. Each day filled with some of the strangest sights, sounds, and especially smells--- seems like a week by itself. And so already I feel like I have been in Andong more than a week. Among the little things that struck me and have more than once caused me no end of chuckles and try to convince myself I am really doing this:

A tiny woman layered in clothes walking nimbly down the muddy road, supporting a huge porcelain pot, at least half as tall as herself on the head, suddenly spots me approaching. Absolute confusion as she can't decide whether to stop and put down the load so she can stare at me. And the old guy with her in the horsehair hat, gray robe, a long white beard, who does stare. They think I look funny?

Twenty-five straight meals with rice—and no end in sight. And it's not just a bite of rice—a whole bowl. Thank God I like the stuff. In two years, that's 2,190 meals of rice!

Forgetting my toilet paper one day—a real catastrophe as often there is nothing to use—learning Koreans consider it very unsanitary to blow the nose in a handkerchief and then putting it back into your pocket (it probably is) and then witnessing their method: right out the nose into the street. Witnessing the morning ritual of washing hands and face: much like a bird bath, water all over the place, very little accomplished in this boy's opinion. Ordering chicken, rice and tea and getting soup and tea. Finding out my co-teacher, who has been teaching English for ten years speaks no English—accepting invitations to three different homes without ever knowing I had accepted one!

Jim found out that the Korean English teachers could only write English; they couldn't speak it. So, he requested and was granted a third year in Korea to teach the teachers to speak English.

An excerpt from a letter dated November 4, 1971:

My co-teacher is now 29: he lived in Taegu or Andong or some other equally provincial place all his life but still I consider him to be the most progressive and modern, if you will, person I know. He speaks English quite well which means he can read Time and Newsweek. He is extremely interested in world politics and we discuss all the current (incredible) events quite often and at great length. He eventually wants to run for the National Assembly.

Anyway, now he's 29 which means Marriage Time in Korea. (always between 27 and 30). So, his mother is on the look; yes, his mother! She is the beautiful old woman who looks like a replica of something from the Yi Dynasty-- a true country person. And, according to tradition, the parents must find the marriage partner. Now in Mr. Lee's case. (my co-teacher) this isn't easy: he's only a little over five feet tall, maybe 5'1" at the most--and of prime consideration in the prospective bride is her height--she must be just a little taller than he--so that their sons (daughters, Heaven forbid) will be tall or taller anyway--but she also can't be too tall or that will look ridiculous.

Now, in. addition to that, she can't be too well educated--rich and well-educated girls are too demanding! But she can't be stupid either. A high school graduate is just right.

Now in order to check all this out, a series of two or three meetings is arranged in a kind of coffee shop. These are the only meetings between the prospective marriage partners--and the mothers of each as well as a go-between are always present. Each meeting lasts about an hour.

In addition to this Mr. Lee does a little "out-side" research on the girls. He has gone to the high school and checked on their records--not only academic, but health-wise too. It is a little like buying a cow at auction: he checks the teeth (must be perpendicular to the jaw, whereas a boy's must be a little protruding, a sign of strength and other health items including the size of her hips (they should be broad so she can deliver a baby easily.) It's really unbelievable.

Then on the basis of this, plus the meetings, the marriage is decided upon! That's it: a couple of hours and the person you're going to spend your life with is chosen. No wonder there is so little family activity in Korea--I mean the family doing things together. Sure, there is all the ceremony--ancient worship, parents honored, etc. But, not once have I ever gone anywhere with a teacher in my school and wife! But, a Korean points out, the divorce rate is nil so who can say?......

(Many years later this couple visited Jim in Boston and me in Villa Rica. The Olympics had brought Korea into the 21st century. Dear people. They have two sons. I'm wearing their gift to me.)

Mr. and Mrs. Yi

When Jim returned from Korea in 1973, he had joined the Catholic Church. The Andong Catholic Church planted a magnolia tree in his honor. I wouldn't have been surprised if he had become a

Buddhist, but I was surprised he had become a Catholic. My family were Presbyterian. Jimmy's parents were Greek Orthodox.

On his return to the U.S., Jim joined the Jesuit Community in Chestnut Hill, Massachusetts and we received this letter from Boston dated:

Monday, 13, February 1978

Hi all:

Just a note to say hello! Have no idea when this might reach you. There's been no mail in or out of Boston for a week. I thought I'd send a couple clippings of what this unbelievable week with the "Storm of the Century" has been like. And then last night we learned about your storm and all the damage there—so maybe this won't seem so bad. I hope all is O.K. in Sierra Madre. Sounds like there was lots of damage in La Crescenta-Tujunga area—but I'm sure you would have called if anything were up at home.

We are still completely closed down—no driving anywhere in the area for an entire week ($500 fine and 1 year in jail for anyone caught driving who isn't "emergency personnel"). Hard to believe that an entire city of 3 ½ million people could close for a week—but we've done it. We're hoping the Governor lifts the ban tonight—but no one knows.

Actually, except for the people who have suffered along the coast, it's been kinda fun—almost a carnival-like atmosphere in the streets---no cars is great! Everybody walking everywhere—for food, etc. But we did begin to go stir crazy after 3-4 days—until they got the subway moving again—I made a beeline for Boston and Cambridge—just to get out!

We have no school again today—the streets are just too narrow for two-way traffic. So, on it goes—it's been a little like a war—a state of siege—the army all over the place helping people. And people have never been nicer to each other. Too bad it takes a disaster to bring this change of attitude about. This morning was the first day business and offices were open again—since last Monday! But you could only go to work if you could walk or take a subway line.

Needless to say, I won't get your anniversary gift to you on time—but don't give up hope. Better late, etc.

Hope you are all well and not too wet!

Much love, Jim

An excerpt from a letter dated 2 December 1979:

Guess what! I'm planning to enter my first swimming meet in 10 years next Sunday. There's a Master's meet at Harvard—I'll be competing in the 30–35-year-old age group—a far cry from the old 13–14 group I was once in! It will be strange swimming the 50-yard butterfly—and maybe the "distance" event of 100 yards! I've only worked out twice this month—and hoping my running will be of some benefit.

Hope all is well with you two!

Love, Jim

When Jim was at Stanford, he competed at the swimming Nationals in Oklahoma and was beaten by Mark Spitz so didn't qualify for the Olympics. Mark Spitz did swim in the Olympics and won nine gold medals, one silver and one bronze.

On a visit to California for a Nickoloff Reunion in 2021, we visited Pasadena High School and saw in the trophy case the big trophy Jim won as Athlete of the Year with his butterfly time still holding the record for the school.

The Jesuits first assignment for Jim was to teach English in Jamaica. His letterhead:

St. George's College
Winchester Park, Kingston, Jamaica,
West Indies

Sunday, 16 November 1980

Hi Mom and Dad from Jamaica!

It's a gorgeous Sunday morning here—about 80 degrees and bright sunshine. The music from Mass is wafting across our school playing field—our school and the Cathedral are right next door to each other.

Well, it's hard to believe I'm here—but I don't have to go very far from my bed to know I'm a long way from home. In many respects Jamaica seems more foreign to me than Korea. Although it's an English-speaking country, the local Jamaican patois is really another language altogether and I'm having trouble understanding a lot of people—especially children and the uneducated people. Of course, Jamaica is 93% black, so that is quite a change from white Boston.

And the country is exceedingly poor—many parts of Kingston look like the poorest parts of Korea. There are cows and goats walking along the streets, even downtown. The food is good, and although we've had plenty to eat here at St. Georgia's, the island, as a whole, is experiencing shortages. This in fact raises moral questions in my mind—it's a little hard to talk with someone you know has only had one meal that day.

The school is much like my experience in Korea only even a little more disorganized. So much of the national life here was disrupted by the last 6-12 months of political turmoil. Some schools are really only now beginning the school year.

My teaching schedule is going to be light, but there will be lots of outside activities. One of the things we're trying to do here at "George's" this year is to begin a program of student ministries—letting the kids know that Christian faith demands more than just private prayer and going to church. We have groups of kids visiting two hospitals, the prison, a home for elderly Chinese people, a boy's home, and a home for deaf kids. I went with a group last week to the Children's Hospital. What an experience—so many poor little kids packed into this place! I don't imagine the medical care is too good—and supper was two slices of bread with some kind of spread on it.

Prices are ridiculous here—gas is $4.65 a gallon. I drove yesterday for the first time—that's a bit exciting because it's on the left, British style. Fortunately, I had Jim Hayes with me to navigate. Between potholes like the Grand Canyon (there are a couple the car could go into but not come out!) the cows, goats and pedestrians and the other traffic, it was harrowing. But I'm leaving on Wednesday, and I have to drive all the way across Kingston alone.

The one thing I should have brought was a mosquito net. The bugs are ferocious at night! There are none available now on the island.

I'm thinking of putting Grandma Lola on this—she's good at things like this.

I really don't think it would be a good idea for them to come at Xmas. There's nothing to see here in Kingston, and though I haven't been to the North Coast yet, I have a feeling things there are the same. Maybe next year after I'm more adjusted.

The mail situation is impossible. Lately Jim Haye's tells me it takes anywhere from 10 days to 3 1/2 weeks to the U.S. and the same time back. A woman is stopping by here this afternoon and she's going to the U.S. tomorrow, so I'll send this with her.

Much love to everybody and
Happy Thanksgiving, Jim

19 December 1980

Hi there!

Miracle of miracles! I went out today and collected —after much red tape and waiting— both the mosquito netting and the check. Thank you, Thank you. It's good to know that some things are possible here—and that I'm not completely cut off.

Thanks especially for the phone call last week-end. That was a great surprise and really picked me up. I'm amazed at how lonely I feel here much of the time. I guess it just takes time— and it's been a long time since I've had to start completely over.

Anyway, I really enjoyed hearing your voices. And having Tom there was a treat. I had been meaning to write him and Dixie to tell them how glad I am to be getting another sister and **HER**! And I'm glad you finally got to go along to Atlanta, Mom. You didn't mention anything about how you liked La Paz one and two, but I'm sure you did.

If this gets to you before Xmas, have a Merry and know that I will be thinking of all of you that day.

Hope all goes well, Much love,

Jim

P.S. Please continue to send U.S. stamps—especially if the price of postage goes up. I'm sending this along with someone going tomorrow to the U.S.

5 February 1981

Surprise! I'm coming to you from California this time. Simon Harak, my sidekick here at "George's" in the Chaplain's office, is leaving tomorrow morning for San Jose of all places. His twin sister is getting married on Valentine's Day, and he'll be the priest witnessing the marriage. (In the R.C. Church the couple marry themselves--that is, they perform the sacrament. The priest simply witnesses as representative of the Church.)

Anyway, I'm taking advantage of his trip to send off a load of mail. It's still impossible here—I got a Xmas card from Irene Moore in Sierra Madre yesterday. She mailed it 22 December—That's almost 7 weeks!

Have some things I want to bring you up on.

1. I got a Christmas card from the Binots (took only 6 days from France!) and she sounded very

excited about the possibility of your going to their home to visit. I hope you can manage it—I know you'd have a great time. Dad would love Le Grand Beauregard and Tours and surroundings. And I'm sure they'd enjoy having you. I, of course, would be intensely jealous.

2. I'm afraid that things are not looking very good for my being able to get up to Atlanta at the end of April. There are all kinds of factors involved here, which I won't go into for the time being, but it's not a good time for me. I only wish the wedding could be in June and then I could be reasonably sure of being able to join you all. But I understand.

(Jim was hoping to go to Tom and Dixie's wedding in Atlanta but he couldn't go.)

Jimmy and I and my mom and Les did visit Jim in Jamaica flying from Atlanta after Tom and Dixie's wedding. We stayed in a house used by visiting nuns. My folks had the bedroom and Jimmy and I slept on single beds under windows on either side of the front door with a fan on a high pole revolving, keeping the mosquitos off of us during the night.

We were warned not to leave anything on the counter in the kitchen because someone could use a pole through the window to steal it. Also, we were not to go outside after 9 p.m. as the guard dogs were loose.

In the middle of the night, we were awakened by blasts of gunfire. Jimmy and I hit the floor. At breakfast, I asked Jim what was happening. He said, "Mom, that happens almost every night. I was just hoping it wouldn't happen last night."

Desperate for teachers, Jim asked his brother John if he would come and help. John did go to Jamaica and teach English at the school. He took the kids to the ocean to see the tide pools. He also organized the boys to paint the peeling buildings and entertained the nuns with his piano playing.

I had been requesting a disk of John playing the piano for years. The only one I have is one he made in Jamaica for my birthday.

15 March 1982

Hi there,

    Will send this to you via some friends going to Boston next Monday, a week from today, but I'm sure it will get to you quicker this way than if I mailed it tomorrow from here. Check out picture and article on page 5. Some people you know! (We're scheduled to do another Colloquium April 1-4). Can't believe that I've made 6 out of 7 issues of The New Catholic Opinion since September when this paper really got underway.

    Jon and I are planning to go out to Maumee this coming weekend, the 19-21. We both need it! He has been working like crazy on a Science Exhibition project and I'm in the stretch now where I'm out 17 or 18 nights in a row. One of these will be a belated birthday dinner at Jon and Tom's on St. Patrick's Day tomorrow night. I can already "taste" the beach at Maumee!

    Hope all is well there. Love, Jim

    Jimmy and I and my folks were present when Jim was ceremoniously ordained a diaconate to the lilting sound of steel drums and local instruments. It took place in a large gymnasium with all the Jamaican Catholics on the island invited.

He gives me songs I can sing,
Church bells that ring
Prayers I can pray
Hope every day….

Chorus: He gives me
All of these things
I'm thinking of
He gives me love.
He gives me love.

He gives me
Wine and my bread
Apples so red,
Mangoes so sweet,
Plenty to eat……
He gives me
Feet I can walk,
Lips I can talk,
Eyes bright and clear
Ears I can hear…….

He gives me
Wine and my bread
Take them he said,
Bread is so sweet,
Take it and eat…….

A month later Jim was ordained a priest at Holy Cross in Worcester, Massachusetts to the sound of trumpets! Jimmy and I and Jim's brothers and Jim's grandparents were all present.

Jim was then sent by the Jesuits to the University of California at Berkeley to earn a PhD in Liberal Theology. At one point he was sent to Bolivia for a summer to learn Spanish and then for several years, he alternated six months in Peru studying the source of Liberal Theology and six months at Berkeley preparing his dissertation.

The following letter came from Bolivia where he was studying Spanish:

INSTITUTO DE IDIOMAS
PADRES DE MARYKNOLL
CASILLA 550
COCHABAMBA—BOLIVIA

14 July 1984. Bastille Day

Hi Everybody,

What a nice surprise to make "radio contact" with you the other night! Nancy suggested that we try, I had my doubts, but she's quite a "pro-fessional amateur" operator and was able to get through a lot of interference to Blair in Burbank. I guess you weren't able to hear me as well or as well as we were able to hear you.

The Quinogas with whom I'm staying are interesting people. As I said, they lived in Miami for six years in the 70's, but because Florida is so Hispanic, they learned little English. They have one 15-year-old son who is adopted. The other night they told me about how hard it's been for them to have children—even by adoption. They had lost 2 or 3 at three months of their own and then went to the US. for medical tests. When it turned out they couldn't have any more, they tried to adopt. The first baby they kept for 4 months before the mother came back and re-claimed her child. A heart-breaking experience. Then they heard via a ham radio operator in Chile who was a doctor that a child was available there.

They went all the way, got the child (their son Rodolfo junior) and almost had him taken away at the border because of a mix-up in papers. When they got back to Bolivia, they adopted a second baby who suffered crib death 4 months later. Hard to believe. So, they stopped with the one boy after 6 attempts. Needless to say, they love him very much. He speaks good English since he lived in the U.S.

It's about a half-hour walk from their house to the Institute. I make the walk four times a day since I come home for the 2-hour lunch we have each day. It's the Spanish system, a small breakfast, a feast at 12:30, and a light supper. The food here is delicious, more interesting, I think, than Colombia. The Quinogas, who have been back in Bolivia for six years now, have had a large number of students from the Language Institute live with them, so they are accustomed to foreigners who can't speak the language very well.

Classes go for four hours in the morning. I have three hours alone with one teacher and one hour in a group of three. After I get back from lunch, I use the language lab for 2 hours and then do an hour more of reading or writing in Spanish. At 5:30 we have Mass—in Spanish for practice. I'm trying to get my nerve up to celebrate a public mass in one of the churches here in Cochabamba, but I'm worried about giving a homily ad lib in Spanish.

The people at the Institute are a fascinating lot. I can't think of a more interesting mix of people I've run across since the old Peace Corps group. Must be those "international types" that I find interesting. There are about 50 students in the Institute now. There's a group of about 10-15 Australians who are wonderful—fun and laughter all the time. There's a priest from L.A. who graduated from La Salle High School in 1966---same age as I am—and lived on Double Drive in Arcadia. He's here learning Spanish so he can work in a Mexican parish in L.A.!

There are two Polish Franciscans (about 30) who just arrived from Poland. Because they speak no English and refuse to speak Russian, we have to converse in Spanish which neither of us knows too well.

Then there's a Swiss girl with whom I speak French. Amazingly enough, one of my favorites among the Aussies spent two years in Korea so we're looking for a Korean restaurant in Bolivia.

And an American seminarian from Long Island, New York who had Jim Lopresti as a teacher, also spent last summer in Korea—and lived and worked with Joe Venerosa in Korea!

It's unbelievable, but almost every person here and I have some little thing like this in common. It's a small world to begin with, but the world of the church is even smaller. Lots of fun to make all these contacts.

As I started to tell you on the radiophone, my trip to Bolivia was very exciting. The morning I was leaving Lima, Peru, for Bolivia, they announced on the radio that the President of Bolivia had been kidnapped and it looked like the beginning of a coup (the 186th in 150 years). So, the Maryknoll priests I was staying with told me that I might not get into Bolivia at all.

However, at the airport we learned that the Bolivian Airline was flying and the flight I was going on would soon arrive from La Paz to make its turn-around. When it arrived, I noticed a large crowd of soldiers and press people and TV cameras—and realized there must be someone important on the plane coming from Bolivia—maybe trying to get out. "What am I getting into? I asked myself.

When the passengers disembarked, this important personage happened to pass near me and stop—and was immediately rushed by the crowd. I had a ring-side seat as they interviewed him—and took a couple of pictures—some cabinet official. After he left saying "No comment" I went to a quiet place in the waiting lounge to sit down and a well-dressed man came up and sat beside me. A few minutes later I looked through the glass partition and noticed the crowd of press and TV people charging toward our waiting room —and sure enough it was he they were after. Turned out he is the Peruvian Ambassador to Bolivia.

    They crowded all around us—just him and me—and kept asking what he thought he'd find when he got to La Paz. He said he had no idea but thought it was safe (which hardly reassured me). They pumped him with all kinds of questions, including trying to find out who <u>I</u> was. He declined to answer most of their questions—and of course, could not shed any light on my identity. I kept my mouth closed.

    When we finally got on the plane, I was exhausted but couldn't go to sleep—partly because of all the excitement (what would I find in Bolivia?) —and partly because of the spectacular scenery outside the window of the plane. I am sure the flight from Lima to La Paz across the Andes must be one of the most spectacular in the world. Huge volcano cones, snow covered ranges, lakes, and tiny villages. Then Lake Titicaca which was like the sea and sits at 12,500 feet in the Andes—and finally La Paz, itself nearly 13,000-foot peaks—spectacular! We were on the ground for an hour at La Paz and I could feel the altitude.

    Arriving at Cochabamba was nice—a clunky little country airport. I was met by John Caleman, *my professor at Berkeley who's also here for the summer studying Spanish and giving a course in theology.*

Cochabamba is very nice—much poorer than Columbia, but a city of gardens and plazas and dust. It's in a wide valley, and the surrounding area looks very much like Palm Springs—dry, rocky mountains in browns and reds and greys. Tunari is the highest peak here at 17,000 ft. Cochabamba is at 8,500 ft. The city is filled with Quechua Indians who speak both Spanish and Quechua. They wear their own costumes—like in Silvia—so it's very colorful.

Hope you are well—lots of love to everybody. Will try to make radio contact again in a few weeks.   Love from Cochabamba, Jim

My 5 o'clock telephone call from Jim tonight lent some more information about the above letter. When Jim arrived at the Bolivian airport, no one came to the plane. People had to fend for themselves, getting their own luggage. The place was deserted. Consequently, Jim never showed his passport to anyone. When he was leaving Bolivia to go to Peru, he decided to go by boat across Lake Titicaca. The immigration authority asked for his passport which did not have a Bolivian arrival visa.

So, the man said he couldn't let Jim leave Bolivia if he hadn't been there. Jim told him "I'm standing right in front of you. Obviously, I'm here." Finally, Jim convinced him that he wouldn't get in trouble to let him leave if he hadn't been there!

Also, I realized that Jim did not know any Spanish before he went to Peru and that is why he was at this institute in Bolivia recommended by his professor from Berkeley, to learn Spanish before he was sent to Peru.

Cochabamba, Bolivia   12 August 1984

Dear Mom,

Happy Birthday from a place high in the mountains and far to the South. I have little hope that this will reach you before you leave for China and even less that it'll make it by your birthday. We are in the middle of a mail strike now—ten days so far and nothing's moving. This is the third major strike in the P.O. since I've been here—a "major" one being more than a week. This place rivals Jamaica!

Still, if and when this reaches you—August, September, October? —it brings best wishes and much gratitude for your life and all you've shared with others of yourself—especially me.

It's a nice coincidence that you're going to Asia upon turning 60—Don't forget that there, sixty represents the completion of one cycle and the beginning of a new time of life. It's like being born again! In Korea they celebrate the 61st year just like the 1st birthday of a child—a big affair. So, both 60 and 61 are important. Wonder what they do in China, the "Center of the Universe" (Middle Kingdom)—maybe you two youngsters will find out?

In case this doesn't make it to you, I'll try to make radio contact once again before I leave the Quinogas. It's been a lot of fun using the radio. You probably found out I talked to Grandma Lola last week. She was great, just like a pro. Nancy couldn't believe how strong her voice sounded. I told her, yes, she is strong and nearly 80!

I spent last week in La Paz. What a fasci-nating city. 1 million people and 12,000 feet above sea level. My window in the S.J. community looked out on Mt. Illimani—magnificent at 21,000 feet. Cold too! Hailed on Thursday and snow at La Paz airport at 14,000 feet, the world's highest major airport. I'm looking forward to Peru—especially Cuzco and Machu

Pichu—but will hate to leave Bolivia. For now, much love and Happy B. Day.

                  (signed) No. 1

Berkeley, 13 September 1984

    Dear Mom and Dad and Patty and Al,

    So how was the Middle Kingdom? You're due to arrive in Beijing today, the 13th and I'm feeling excited for you. Hope weather, service, etc., and all those "little things" are cooperating to allow you to enter fully into the experience of China!

    Got a note from you yesterday in which was enclosed your itinerary. I would have written earlier from South America, so that you'd have a letter waiting in some exotic port of call, but I knew none of your addresses. I won't make this long since I have little guarantee that it will reach you even in Hong Kong—but just want to let you know that I've made it back to the North American mainland (even if everyone else seems to have left for other parts).

    It was a fantastic summer (winter, that is) and extremely profitable from both the academic and spiritual points of view. In the week I had in

Lima, Peru, I was able to make a number of important contacts and set some things up for the possibility of a year's research there in 1986. Visited the main center where liberation theologians are working, and they offered me office space and the use of their library collection—very friendly.

By far, the highlight of the time in South America was the trip I made from La Paz to Cuzco and Machu Pichu by land (and sea!) Luis had been doing research in Lima and he flew to La Paz where we met. From there we took a bus to Lake Titicaca—itself 12,500 ft. high in the Andes.

Landscape is stark—above the tree line for the most part—and beautiful. We crossed Lake Titicaca by boat into Peru and continued on to the region of the altiplano where Mary Ann Clifford, Luis's cousin, is working. Unfortunately, she was not there having just arrived back in Lima after surgery in the U.S. But through friends of hers we were able to get an inside view of the Indian life and culture there.

From there we took a train to Cuzco and on to the lost city of the Incas—Machu Pichu. It has to be seen to be believed—hauntingly beautiful—absolutely remote and isolated. I felt a strange urge to come back some day and spend more than a day. It's so lost in the clouds that you feel like you could just step into heaven from the Inca stone ruins. God is near.

Stopped a few days in Cali (Columbia) to help Luis' pack up baggage to California. His father and mother were extremely curious about your travel to China. Don't think they'd ever consider such a step into the unknown, but Lucho kept asking me a million questions about China, etc. They send their love.

Got back to Berkeley to find out I'd been moved out of Virginia Street! The Jesuits had an overflow this year of students—so six of us were put in apartments on the other side of the University campus. So now I'm organizing a new household.

Hope all is well with the four of you. Rest up in Hong Kong and enjoy the exotic sights in Thailand and Singapore. Love to you all, JBN

When a person becomes a priest, he returns to his hometown to give his first sermon. Jim was going to assist Luis at his first mass in Cali, Columbia. Luis invited Jimmy and me to attend, also. When we hesitated, Luis sent us a postcard saying that the whole country of Columbia is awaiting our arrival and his aunt wants to play golf with us. With that,

Jimmy said, "Well I guess if the whole country is awaiting our arrival, we better go."

We flew Eastern Airlines to Miami and Avianca to Columbia. There was a plaque hanging over the plane isle that said the Pope had blessed this plane in 1956. Since this was 1983, I hoped his blessing was still in force.

Obviously, we made it and had a wonderful time with Luis family and playing golf with his aunt. The only time I've ever played with my own caddy! They also took us up into the Andes where they had a vacation home. The women and men were wearing fedora hats and the ladies ten or more strings of beads around their necks. The young boys wore high laced boots with the laces untied—typical boys!

Mom and Andes ladies

Berkeley 5 January 1985

Dear Mom and Dad,

Thanks for a great time—Christmas Eve church, big Xmas day, day or at least afternoon skiing on the slopes, visit to Grandpa in Palm Springs, day in Sierra Madre and Los Angeles and dinner at Jon's—we did it all! Saw the Sierra Madre float on T.V. just tuned in at the right time. Didn't look too bad in black and white.

Thought you might enjoy the enclosed piece about chopsticks. I don't care what they do in China— "we" Koreans will never give the sticks up! Food does taste better with 'em.

All for now, Jim

Ciudad de Mexico, 29 July 1985

Dear Mom and Dad,

I'm almost at the mid-point of my stay in Mexico—and have begun to settle into a routine. As I mentioned in my card to you, the trip from San Diego to La Paz, nearly the length of Baja, was a bit rough—very hot (probably over 100 degrees all the way), long bus rides for two days (and one night) although we stopped in Loreto on

Gulf coast one night, little in the way of comfort (food, mosquitos, etc.).

The hardest thing was finding out it was next to impossible to get tickets for the ferry to Mazatlán! After 3 hours of waiting and cajoling, I managed to acquire 3 tickets for us---but no cabin space, so we had to spend the night on the steel floor of the ship's deck—a 17-hr. ride, quite pretty really, except I was exhausted.

My two traveling companions, Bob Eidinger and Kery Vrabel, both 10 years younger than I am, had little trouble – so—I think the moral is: I'm getting old! I remember doing such things 10 to 15 years ago—overnight on the floor of a ferry from Pusan to Japan—no trouble at all. I guess my days of roughing it are over.

It was such a relief to get to Guadalajara which is not only a dreamlike jewel of a city, but at 5000 feet nice and cool--as well as very civilized (=comfortable). Many Americans have retired there. We did very civilized things—i.e., went to a dance performance in a lovely theater, ate in beautiful restaurants, had a shower! Guadalajara is a fascinating city, filled with lovely plazas, churches, art, etc.

The trip from Guadalajara to Mexico City is nine hours, but the bus was comfortable and the scenery beautiful—lots of green, almost like Colombia. I was surprised and relieved (after moon-like Baja California)—and the time passed quickly. The mountains and farms of Central Mexico plus little colonial churches here and there are charming.

Mexico City, the Big Enchilada, is incredible. I'm sure there are things that are unchanged since you were here nearly 40 years ago—the main plaza, the Colonial section, etc. (Jimmy and I had our honeymoon in Mexico.) But the largest avenue, La Paseo de la Reforma, is lined with big, modern buildings, very pretty with trees, etc. and the sheer size of the city is daunting. They now say it's hit 18 million people, making it the second largest urban area after Tokyo.

It has a magnificent metro system—clean, quiet, with music—and the ride costs only ¼ cent. I use it all the time. The problem, of course, is that everyone else does too!

The cultural possibilities here are amazing—museums, concerts, libraries, etc. It's like New York—and in fact, most people (outside of Mexico too) say that it's the capital of the whole Spanish-speaking world (including Spain) in terms of publishing, writing, art, business, etc. It's an exciting place to be and also a cultural melting pot. They keep finding more and more Aztec ruins buried under this city as they build more and more. Mexico is very self-consciously Indian—unlike Colombia which ignores its indigenous population or Peru which oppresses its.

Work here in Los Angeles parish is proceeding apace. I usually celebrate either the morning or evening mass (or both) and take time to hear confessions (which can be funny since I don't always understand everything the person says, especially if he or she has no teeth. But I know God hears, understands, and forgives, and that's all that matters!)

I've also gone to give the last rites to the dying—and have thus been able to get inside some of the poor houses that make up this parish. It's very humbling—and the people are warm, kind, and grateful. They call me "padrecito Jaime."

Our Jesuit community is poor as well—we don't eat very well or live very ostentatiously. But they're extremely good men—quite knowledgeable and hard-working.

My room is simple and cold. At 7500 feet it never gets hot here, in fact, it rains almost every day in the afternoon. I have ample time for my own work. I'm gathering material in Spanish on Gustavo Gutierrez and trying to work my way through it in preparation for next year in Peru.

Two theologians live here in the house—so I have some help. No one really speaks English, so I get lots of practice in Spanish.

As I told you before I left, my plans are to leave here for Los Angeles on August 22 (Thursday,) and then spend the weekend with you for Mom's birthday (first time in years, I'm sure.) However, there are two things I need to straighten out. (Arranging for his brother John to pick him up on arrival.)

Lots of love from Mexico,
Jim
New address: Apartado 3090, Lima Peru

13 August 1986

Dear Mom,

A quickie note and birthday greeting that I want to send with someone who's leaving for Los

Angeles tonight. The mail seems to be getting more irregular again. I got your letter--sounds like things are coming to a conclusion with the house. Felicidades! (Congratulations).

I got Betty Nickoloff's invitation to Grandpa's B-day party. Sure wish I were closer! If you'd like, maybe you could give me a call from the party. I could greet Grandpa, you and Jac all at once! I sent a card to Grandpa but who knows when it will arrive. Betty said the dinner's at 1 p.m. there.

If you called about 2 p.m. (which is 4 p.m. here—two-hour difference), I'd be home from an early afternoon appointment I have. In any case, I'll be at this number from 4 pm on—81-46-67. That's my home number. I'd call you but it's much harder (and more expensive)—takes up to 5 hours to put a call through from here.

In any event, I hope the party is happy for all. And hope you're in your new house by then!

Lots of love,

Jim

P.S. I'm leaving Lima for the altiplano on Aug. 25 (your B-day) to September 5. I need to see the sun! I've been staying with Mary Ann and two friends up there. Br-r-r-r 13,000 feet, but sunny during the day.

El Rimac, Lima, 13 October 1986

Dear Mom and Dad,

Your nice fat letter arrived, filled with news in word and picture of all that's been going on there. I guess because I'm beginning to feel more at home here, but also because family and friends have been such good correspondents, I feel less far away than I did the first two months. Thanks for your moral support.

The photos are proof that the house turned out beautifully, a real work of art. It's almost as if years' worth of faded magazine and newspaper clippings about house building and decorating had been turned into a physical reality in your home—to say nothing of the little touches that could only have come from you, Mom. I feel that my "place" in the house is assured in that some of my own things have been given a place of honor (or to put it another way, I don't see how you could eliminate a couple of those Korean works of art without having to start decorating all over again!)

I am eager to see it all, though August next year is still a long way off. I am especially anxious to try the garden bath. I have tried out your suggestion of thinking of that lovely place while standing under the cold shower here in the morning, but frankly, it doesn't help. I still freeze. Oh, summer, please get here fast! I have shown the photos to a couple of U.S. friends here, but although Peruvians are not quite as proper as Asians, I'm not sure what they would think of my parents posing in their underwear, even if it was August!

    I'm glad you have enjoyed my letters so far. You say they call to mind the time I was in Korea, and I think that's right, for in some ways this experience is similar, though different in important ways too. The main differences have to do, I am sure, with the changes I have undergone in the nearly 13 years since I left Korea. My life is much more clearly defined now than it was then. There I was like a free-floating agent, open to whatever came along. Here I have a position of responsibility—after just a couple of months—and a very definite purpose in being here, i.e., to do the research for and part of the writing of my dissertation.

    I don't have the time to go galivanting around the countryside in quite the same way (or style) I did in Korea. But in many ways this time in Peru calls to mind days in Andong. I think one of the great disappointments in Jamaica, and maybe an important reason I had no desire to stay there a long time was the fact that it's "in English." I have to admit that I like the challenge of another language and a culture which is equally distinct. Since I've moved here to Gustavo's parish, I can go days without speaking or hearing a word of English.

The other day I spoke with my friend Jim Lopresti by radio and he noted that my English didn't seem to have deteriorated too much. I told him that yes, it has, and although my Spanish has been improving little by little, I think overall there's been a net loss—more English lost than Spanish gained!

When I say that I'm "established" now in a position of responsibility, I'm referring to the fact that with Gustavo's two-month long absence in the US, I am really pastor of the parish now. This has been very good for me, especially in terms of getting to know the people and their faith, but there is also a tension between this pastoral involvement and the primary responsibility I have here which is my dissertation.

What is happening is that the people here are coming to like me and want me to be part of things more and more—inviting me to all kinds of things—and of course I like this since it is such a welcome change from the first two months here when I was alone and isolated in the main Jesuit community downtown. Now I have no shortage of things filling my calendar. But this is beginning to conflict with my study time, something Gustavo warned me about. If I'm not careful, I could get involved up to my neck with things here in the parish—and have nothing written on the theology of Gustavo Gutierrez come next June.

In the last week alone, for example, I was asked to hear a number of confessions since October is the holist month in Lima—the fiesta of Our Lord of the Miracles—and the whole city is going through a time of purification, with many people dressed in purple, the color of penance. But in addition to this, I was asked to lead the blessing of a new fried chicken restaurant two blocks away, and to go with about 200 parishioners on a family outing day to a nearby park. Both events were fun and very meaningful at the same time (but also time-consuming).

The fried chicken blessing was great-- believe it or not I had never been to a restaurant opening before in my life—not in Hollywood, Sierra Madre, Atlanta or anywhere else! This was quite a formal affair, flowers everywhere, champagne and of course, music, good food, and about 150 people. The blessing was the highlight and since there's nothing in the prayer book about fried chicken, I had to make it up as I went.

What they really wanted was lots of prayers and lots of water thrown all over everything and everyone from the floor to the ceiling, from the painting of the Sacred Heart of Jesus in the dining room to the sinks in the kitchen. They all told me it was a beautiful ceremony, and their deep religiosity made me think of Asia as well. It's like the spiritual dimension pervades everything here—kind of like in Japan or Korea, it's part of the air people breathe. The funny part was the next day when many people stopped me on the street and said, "Oh Padre, that was a wonderful ceremony last night at the chicken restaurant"—and these were people who weren't even there. News travels fast in this barrio.

Yesterday was the family outing day and although it took my whole day, I was glad to be part of it. We went to a large regional park about 15 minutes north of here but still very much in the middle of Lima. The drive up there was incredible—it's just amazing how huge this city is, and how poor, and how barren.

Mile after mile of shacks or just the beginnings of houses (a few bricks, electricity perhaps), up and down the gray hillsides which don't have a blade of grass on them. In a way it's a miracle that Lima exists at all. It's much drier than your Mojave Desert. The park itself wasn't too bad, with some grassy areas and lots of basketball courts, etc. We started with mass and then moved into games that everybody could participate in—or most everybody, since so many people here have suffered from polio and are permanently crippled.

Then we had lunch, and of course everybody wanted to give me some of theirs, which was nice since I forgot to bring anything along and there was no place to buy anything to eat. The best part was the sudden and unexpected appearance of the sun. That makes about 2 days of sunshine we've had now in the last three weeks—not too bad. I think the fog bank along the coast may be beginning to break up at long last.

After lunch some of the little kids went to a section of the park where there are rides, and one little kid, Carlos, wanted me to go along with him. Carlos is one of my favorites here, not only because he's such a nice kid (9 years old) but also because I know his family background. His mother is a prostitute—the only way she can support her children and they live in a hovel just behind our church. The building would be condemned in a minute at home.

I knew why Carlos wanted me to go along with him because he didn't have the 6 cents it costs to get into the rides. I was happy to help him take part with all the other kids, but it really turned into an emotional experience for me because when we got to the area where the rides are, I could see just how poor Lima really is. The rides were almost pathetic—ready to fall apart, I'm sure—set against the background of a barren mountain with shacks rising as high as they could go.

But what really got to me was how happy the kids were, and especially Carlos. When he got on board this little airplane ride—so broken down that the planes almost didn't get off the ground--he had the biggest smile on his face, and he continued beaming the whole time waving at us each time he went around. I tried to smile back but the tears just rolled down my face. I kept thinking of the times my little group of friends in Sierra Madre went to Disneyland in the summer. This is the part of Peru that hurts.

Living in Lima is easy for very few people, if anyone. Just trying to get from one place to another on a bus is a major undertaking, given the cattle car conditions, the irregular schedules, and the constantly changing routes. One is tempted to think occasionally that this is the way things are here in Latin America and that it really doesn't bother the locals all that much. Well, the indignities endured daily by Limenos do not mean that people ever get used to them.

I love the story that Gustavo told me about the time he was traveling back to Lima from Miami on Air Panama and was unceremoniously dumped in Panama City for an unscheduled 8-hour wait—this, after a host of other abuses by the airline, was the last straw. So up he went to the ticket counter and very calmly and respectfully said to the senorita working there, "Excuse me, but could you possibly tell me if Air Panama makes a distinction between passengers and luggage?

"I'm sorry, sir, I'm not sure I understand what you mean" replied she. Gustavo repeated the question very civilly: "Yes, I would like to know if your airline makes a distinction between the passengers and the baggage or do they both get the same treatment?" Seeing the light, she became defensive murmuring, "Yes... well, sir, if you'd like to register a complaint, you may fill out this form here." The way Gustavo tells the story in a serious tone of voice is hilarious.

I'm going to have to close this letter. I'll be sending it along with my friend Steve Judd, friend who is in the same doctoral program in Berkeley but who has worked in Peru as Maryknoll priest for ten years and has opened a lot of doors for me. He is leaving this weekend to go back to Berkeley to finish writing his own dissertation. So, I'll send several letters with him, just to make sure they get there. I tried to call you and Grandma by radio last weekend, but no one was home.

I'm sure you're enjoying the arrival of fall, and in your new house. Here it's spring we're grateful for. It's funny, but since virtually every day has been the same since I got here at the end of May—dark, cold fog—I have had no sense of the passage of time. This is further complicated by the fact that the seasons are reversed here. So I feel totally confused and try not to forget that when people talk about something happening in the summer, they mean January. It helps me realize that everything in this universe is relative.

Love from Lima,

Jim

In a recent phone call from Jim, he told me that it had not rained in Lima for 500 years. The whole town is not only covered with grey fog but also covered with layers of dust. They get their water from the Amazon River.

This next letter to my Mom and Les may be a bit repetitious, but it really describes life in Lima.

El Rima, Lima. 14 October 1986

Jon's 37th birthday

Dear Grandma and Les,

First of all, a very happy birthday to you, Gram! I'm going to try to stay on top of things this year and remember everybody's birthday like I used to do and not get so overrun with things that I forget. So I'm aware today of Jon and of your b-day coming up. Since a friend of mine will be traveling to the US this week-end, I'll take advantage of his trip to send this along.

I thought it might be interesting for you if I detailed a typical day for me here, since in some respects this "adventure" is as unusual for me as Korea. Besides I know that you are always interested in all the little details of my life, and I appreciate this since I like to share them.

I thought it might be interesting for you if I detailed a typical day for me here, since in some respects this "adventure" is as unusual for me as was Korea. To begin with, this bed I wake up in in the morning is a bit make-shift since the bed that was here in the room when I arrived in Gustavo's parish was made for him or the other members of the team of three who work here. The problem is that Gustavo is under 5 feet tall, and Sister Maria Luisa is even shorter, and Fr. Juan is the shortest or all. It's like being with three Mr. Yi's in Korea. I feel like the giant of Jack and the Beanstalk, and at first I thought that you had to be under a certain height to work here!

Anyway, the beds and everything else fit these small people, so we had to improvise a new bed for me. Since I like a hard bed, that wasn't too hard—just a few boards nailed together and then a thin mat on top of it—again something like Korea. I usually wake up at 5:30 mostly because of the traffic which starts at 5:00 when the nightly curfew from 1 to 5 ends. It's not only vehicular either—mostly pedestrians who are plying the streets on their way to work —or already working as street vendors. There are several kinds of horns and clappers which are used to indicate what it is they are coming by with-- the fresh bread man squeezes a bicycle-like horn, the person with milk blows a flute, the knife sharpener announces himself with a sharp whistle almost like a tea kettle boiling, the bottle and glass collector claps a wooden spoon against a bottle, and so forth. It's really quite interesting--and they come by all during the day, but especially in the morning. Perhaps the most important sound is that of a cowbell which announces the arrival of the garbage collector. At the sound of the bell, the people start running out of their houses carrying bags of trash from all directions. There is no regular day or time for collection service—could be any time from 5 am to 12 midnight, but it is quite a sight when they arrive and the people dash into the streets from all sides.

Because the weather is cold, damp, and nasty every morning, I usually prepare myself a bowl of hot cereal for breakfast. This is after I do my exercises and go for my run three mornings a week to a park about a mile and half away. Some kids here in the parish go with me to run. My breakfast cereal is an original concoction made of things available here: I use oats as the base and add wheat germ, bran, dried soy, chopped nuts and raisins. I cook this in hot milk—and presto, in 5 minutes I have a delicious meal with my fresh roll and slices of orange. Sometimes before and some-times after I eat, I shave and shower—in cold water since there are few places in Lima that have hot water (the

Jesuit community downtown where I lived for the first two months has hot water showers, so that was something I gave up by moving here to Rimac to live with Gustavo, but the trade-off has been well worth it. I try not to feel too virtuous when I emerge from another cold blast of the shower. In any event, it really wakes you up, and if you can survive the first 30 seconds which are an agony, it's not too bad—kind of refreshing actually.)

About 8 :30 I hit my desk, and I try to study straight through till 12:30 to get in 4 good hours of study at the beginning of the day since the afternoons and even more the evenings seem to fill up so easily with countless things to take care of. If I get good study time in in the morning, I don't feel so bad if the rest of the day kind of "falls apart." Around 12: 30 I go out to the market to get what-ever I need—fresh fruit, the newspaper, powdered milk, a part for something that has broken, etc. The market is outdoors—very much like Korea—really it is just an open space along the highway which passes about 4 blocks from here, where the people set up their tables and stalls at 5:30 a.m. and are there till about 2 in the afternoon. On Sat and Sun they are there all day. It's a fascinating place to walk through—all kinds of things for sale, I especially enjoy the big baskets of different grains and beans for sale—bright beautiful colors, I hope to learn more about. Cooking some of these things, but for now I have only an electric frying pan (Teflon), which was a gift to Gustavo, to cook on as our electric hot plate conked out. I have a tiny fridge—holds less than one shelf of your box does. As a friend said, it dates from the year I. I'm just hoping against hope that it holds out till Gustavo gets back from the US in mid-December.

At 1 pm I wander over to Senora Maria's house down the street to pick up my lunch. She supports her family—children, mother—by cooking for a number of people around here including me. Lunch is always the main meal in Latin America. For me that means a soup—usually quite hearty with vegetables and pieces of chicken, rice, meat, cooked vegetables and all covered with a hot sauce. Peruvian food is quite spicy and I like it a lot. This daily lunch costs me about 60 cents. You can't beat the price or the love that comes with the food.

Around 2 o'clock I head out for the afternoon.

Usually I walk to the theological Institute which Gustavo founded about 1 5 years ago. It's about 12 blocks away. They have an excellent library and most of the resources I need for here in Lima-- as opposed to being in Berkeley—is that the reality all around me is the very thing I'm reading about Gustavo's theology—namely the struggle of the poor for survival, for their rights, for changes in this society and the role of their Christian faith and of the church in this process of social transformation. In the morning when I'm sitting at my desk, I look right out the window at the broken hopes and dreams of so many people who nevertheless find meaning in life and find much to celebrate too. This mixture of poverty and generosity and faith is quite striking. When I walk to the Institute, it's the same thing: I have to pass by scenes of misery and conditions unfit for human beings to live in—and yet they manage to survive. It's almost a miracle. Reading about this reality from the comfort of the library in Berkeley is one thing: reading while living the reality—or at least trying to get a little closer to it—is quite another.

I return from the Institute around 5:30 pm and usually have a meeting here in the parish at 7 or 8. Since I eat lunch so late—always after I and sometimes it's nearly 2--I'm not too hungry at 6. But if I have a meeting that's going to go till 10, I try to fix myself a little sandwich, some cheese, etc. before I go downstairs to the meeting. I am part of two groups here in the parish--the Christian Workers Group, and the Bible Reflection Group, which meet on Mondays and Fridays. But there are always other things to take care of too, so nearly every night there's something. I take Wednesdays off and go off with some Australian priest friends who have a car so some-times we even get out of the city altogether. The other day that is a bit different, of course, is Sunday when I usually have both the 8 am and the 7: 30 pm masses to celebrate. This involves having to prepare a homily in Spanish, something I'm getting better at doing. At least the people claim to be able to understand me—so that's good to know.

When I finish with my evening activities, usually around 10 pm or so, I come back upstairs to the apartment and watch the news while I eat some yogurt mixed with fresh fruit--apples, oranges, whatever I have. I try to get to bed before 11 but sometimes there's so much noise out on the street that I can't go right to sleep. The problem is that people here live in such crowded conditions—a whole family of 5 or 6 often lives in one room, and the houses are jammed together so that the only place to get a little space is on the street. Everybody in Lima lives most of their life on the street—and unfortunately one of the nicer places to sit around here happens to be the steps of the church, right under my window. The thing that saves me is the curfew. I always know that by 1 am at the latest people will be off the streets. Besides I have my ear plugs which have saved me many hours of sleeplessness.

So that's what a typical day is like for me. It's a routine I basically like broken up by unexpected events, good and bad. Sometimes someone comes to visit from the mountains or from other parts of Lima, and this is always a welcome change in the routine. Other times something goes wrong—everything mechanical here seems to break down constantly. This can be an aggravation.

I'm going to sign off now, hoping you are both well, that your birthday celebration is happy, and that you are adjusting to your new home like I'm trying to do here in mine. There's one little thing you could do for me if you get a chance. It's funny but although Peru has plastic bags—indeed, nearly everything comes in plastic bags, including fresh milk, cereal, all kinds of things, they don't have those little wire ties that we use to close the bag again after you open it. I wonder if you could stick a couple in the envelope the next time you write—I'm referring to the small ones, not the big thick ones used to tie up vegetables, but the ones used to tie up a plastic trash bag. Just put a couple in the envelope and I think they will arrive OK. Thanks,

Much love to you both, JBN

Lima, 9:50 am 15 December 1986

Dear Friends,

Especially Grandma Lola and Les

Christmas-fiesta approaches and with it the beginning of summer in the South of our world. Much around me in Lima really does make me feel like I'm standing on my head looking at the world from a different angle: a world where the desperately poor are the vast majority and not a too-easy-to-forget fraction; where it never rains but is damp and grey almost all the time; where cultures and ways of life separated by centuries and continents clash every day in the streets even though everyone is "Peruvian," "Catholic" and a "child of God"; where theology is inevitably politics and politics the incarnation of faith; where everything important happens in Spanish (except my private pleas to God).

Not all is unfamiliar in these surroundings: friendship is born and grows, often unexpectedly, a mystery, but always welcome; reality turns out to be a good deal more complex than a first (or second or third) glance would indicate; and life is time spent loving God--and washing clothes, preparing food, sweeping my room, travelling on buses, attending meetings.

Seven months of the unexpected and the ordinary in Lima. I arrived at the end of May, plans in hand for a year's research and writing on liberation theology in the "movement's" birthplace.

Last April a careful reading of the major texts seemed a good preparation. Yet could one ever be "ready" for Lima where the texts' frequent references to "an unjust and oppressive social reality" turn out to be an overwhelming panorama of human misery and death in all its forms? I guess I could not have been "ready" to face the question of who God is in Lima--loving, just, present? A disorienting and dark question--and (at least for me) one not settled simply, once and for all.

But neither could I have anticipated Gustavo Gutierrez's invitation in late July to move to the parish where he lives and works--a move which rescued me from the anonymity of Lima's vastness, put me smack dab in the ambiente of the theological. Nicest of all is the gradual interweaving of lives in which one ceases to be a menacing stranger and instead becomes, with all my peculiarities, just another brother in a family of special people.

It is no news that life is a struggle and frequently painful, even if truth, justice, and love are worth the fight. What I already knew has been confirmed in Lima. Yet it is news--good news master himself, and offered me instant pastorship (Peruvian style--community leads the way) of the church of Cristo Redentor during Gustavo's lengthy absences. Talk about standing on your head --every time people find a way to celebrate, to party, to feast along the way, even amid the sorrows. People here, like people at home, have the gift of fiesta. More than an escape from a world where life is threatened on every side, fiesta is the re-creation of life at the heart of this world. **FELIZ NAVIDAD**--Happy Re-birth. Here's to you across the miles!

 Lots of love, JBN

    Berkeley 18 March 1987
 Dear Ones,

  It's great to be back on this coast (although come to think of it, I was on this same coast in Peru—Oh well.). Bought my ticket today for Apple Valley. Can hardly wait. I arrive in Ontario on Alaska #122 at 12:15 p.m. Tuesday, April 14. See you then! Leave on April 21 at 12:31 p.m. All for $58.00. I'm looking forward to Easter in Apple Valley (like olden days in Palm Springs.)

Have a good time in the mountains in Arizona.

Love, Jim

4 July 1987

Dear Mom and Dad,

The big news here is that I'm going to have to change my plans for returning home. I had a feeling this might be the case, but I wanted to see what the prospects might be. It now looks like I might be here through August since the part of the dissertation I'm in is presenting problems I didn't count on and there's a whole new section I'll have to do.

The other day I sat down and figured out my time—and felt a little nervous as I could see the October 1 deadline approaching. With so little time remaining I could (can) feel the weight of the three years' work this project presents. And I have to finish because Holy Cross says my contract is conditional upon completing all PhD requirements by Nov. 1. Part of the problem is getting time with Gustavo who's extra-busy these days because of the extremely critical situation here in both the Church and the country. This situation, of course, makes my dissertation only that much more interesting to people in the U.S. (and Peru, too)—and it looks like there might be a good chance of getting it published.

    But in the meantime, bringing it to birth is turning out to be a harder task than I bargained for. Some days I'm ready to throw in the towel which I know would be foolish after all this. But my psychic and creative energies are down, that's for sure. I know this experience of delay and exhaustion is common to the dissertation process (remember Jac?) and I don't know if I'd do it over again if I had to decide. But that's where I am.

    This means I'll miss the reunion on the 30th which I'm sorry about—mostly because I wanted to see our family, all the boys, etc. and the kids.

    P.S. Had a nice thing happen the other day. Because of the pressure on Gustavo now from Rome and from the Peruvian bishops who are mostly reactionaries, we're trying to get a statement of gratitude published in honor of Gustavo's 60th birthday this year and signed by bishops from around the world—to show there is a lot of support for him.

When I was asked if I knew any bishops personally, I remembered Bishop Dupont in Andong—so got right on the phone. Took me three days to track him down, but when I finally did, it was worth it. He was as gracious as ever, said yes, he'd read Gustavo's works (in Korean translation) and would be happy to sign.

He wanted to know when I could go to Korea to see them and give lectures on liberation theology. Just hearing his voice and hearing about people there took me right back. It also confirmed my hope that this Church isn't a lost cause yet!

Interesting to note that most of Jim's letters from Peru were postmarked on the outside of the envelope with cities all over the U.S. depending on where the person lived bringing them to be mailed. Just like in Jamaica.

Lima 100, Peru. 28 October 1987

Dear Mom and Dad,

Just a note to take advantage of a friend's trip to Los Angeles this evening to send this note along. According to people here, the mail service is still pretty unreliable.

Just want to let you know that I arrived safe and sound and have been settling in fine. I had no trouble getting my computer things through customs, Thank God, and have been given office space at the Jesuit residence downtown where I have everything set up. I'll be using their printer.

I'm living with Gustavo again in the parish. The people have welcomed me back warmly. My routine is to go to my "office" nearly every day from about 9-5. In early morning and most evenings after 8, I'm in the parish though occasionally I spend a night out of Lima.

Things are pretty much the same here. Almost feels like I was never away. Weather is slightly better—we've already seen the sun a couple of times which is a hopeful sign! Hope you are all well.

Lots of love, Jim

Lima, Peru 2 December 1987

Dear Friends,

A year has passed since I last wrote you from Peru—a year of the unexpected. Last year at Christmas time the struggle for survival with dignity by the overwhelming mass of Peruvians in the face of extreme and worsening poverty formed the context of life, work, and prayer. In late January the context shifted as I had to return to the U.S. due to illness (typhoid and assorted viruses) and begin an 8-month period of recuperation.

It was difficult to leave Lima because of those who had befriended me, both in the parish where I live and work and study with (liberation theologian) Gustavo Gutierrez, preparing my dissertation of his ecclesiology, and in the foreign community of missionaries in Peru. The context changed, but in a strange way, I discovered a deeper solidarity with Peru and its people, for illness may be one of the few ways that we from the First World can know —from the inside—a central feature of poor people's daily experience, namely, vulnerability and the inability to control life. In such straits one may discover a stronger, and more real, kind of faith. I hope I have.

Yet the months of recovery at home—in Boston and Berkeley—held unexpected gifts as well. Not only did each month seem to bring the gladness of savoring old friendships, the surprise of new ones, the care of Jesuit brothers, and the pleasure of the family table, but love took on new meaning as God asked for words of farewell at the death of three dear people in my life—Mary Beth of Philadelphia, Al of Bakersfield, and Les, whose love for my brothers and me surpassed that of a step-grandfather. The loss we all feel is great, yet for me the love and goodness of these people is even greater, and in the end, I yield in wonder at the mystery of having known, loved, and been loved by each of them. Surely, they revealed the face of God to me.

In mid-October during the immense celebration in Lima of Senor de los Milagros (Lord of the Miracles)—two million people in the streets as the icon-image passes—I returned, miraculously, to luminous faith and spirited theology, glad to take up again with people here whose hearts house love and courage, and who really are about the business of building a new Church--and a new society into the bargain, appearances to the contrary notwith-standing. Time this trip will be short—just till March when I hope to have finished three chapters of my writing—but long enough to taste again the joy of being a brother of some of God's chosen ones. May the God of Life come to birth again and join us across the miles. Feliz Navidad to you.

Lima. 4 July 1988

Dear Mom and Dad,

The big news here is that I'm going to have to change my plans for returning home. I had a feeling this might be the case, but I wanted to see what the prospects might be. Now it looks like I might be here through August since the part of the dissertation I'm in is presenting problems I didn't count on, and there's a whole new section I'll have to do.

The other day I sat down and figured out my time—and felt a little nervous as I could see the October 1 deadline approaching. With so little time remaining I could (can) feel the weight of the three years' work this project represents. And I have to finish because Holy Cross won't let me teach in January until I finish the dissertation.

Berkeley, California, 2 December 1988

Dear friends and Mom and Dad,

For the first time in three years, I find myself north of the Equator in this season of hope and expectation. Temperatures drop and days shorten here, while in Peru, where I spent most of 1988, the opposite is true. Moving between worlds does more than spice up one's life; I have learned that it can significantly affect your vision, desires, and choices.

A year of blessing, 1988 divides for me into three parts, each marked by an important personal milestone. From January to mid-August, I continued to live and work in Lima, where uncommon friends—Peruvians and foreigners alike—shared with me their lives of faith and commitment to justice for the poor, providing the context for the dissertation in theology I was writing. Turning 40 in February allowed for a first-time summer birthday party. Though friends sought to console me on the occasion, my own reaction—in view of all that life has packed into these years—is amazement that I'm **ONLY** 40.

I reached a more important milestone in Lima. When I made the decision to seek to return to Peru to work after completing graduate studies. Several strands of my personal journey seem to come together in Peru—cross-cultural fascination, political commitment, and religious faith. Peru represents a mixture of the Amerindian world of the descendants of the Incas (themselves a distant reflection of Asia), Europe, and Africa.

It is also a land where political savvy contrasts sharply with the general apathy in the U.S. This child of the '60's feels more at home in some ways in such an ambience. But the reality of massive, inhuman poverty also engages one spiritually, challenging traditional concepts of Church as well as of society. For me personally, Peru means correcting a tendency to the abstract, the idealistic and the transcendental by embracing the concrete world of human suffering with realism.

Despite my desire to return to Peru, the Jesuits have asked me to take a teaching job at Holy Cross College in Worchester, Massachusetts beginning in January in order to share with college students some of what I have learned in Latin America. Though I miss Peru already. I look forward to this work of "reverse mission," and will take seriously the need to change North American ways of thinking and acting and to establish relationships of justice with other peoples. (My address after January will be College of the Holy Cross, Worcester, MA 01610; telephone 508-793-2011

I returned to Berkeley in mid-August to complete the doctoral program, a happy event concluded (somehow appropriately) on Halloween when I defended my thesis on the concept of

Church at work in the theology of Gustavo Gutierrez. Gustavo is the founder of liberation theology with whom I lived and worked in Lima. Thus, came to an end a five-year project and the beginning of a welcome break in November and December.

May God who is the Friend of Life, surprise us all again in this season with a rebirth of hope, justice, and love. Merry Christmas to you,

With lots of love and thanks, Jim

Jim's dissertation was published in 1996: *Gustavo Gutierrez Essential Writings.*

The letter below was written on the back of a birthday card for mothers in Spanish for my 65th birthday:

Lima, 15 August 1989

Dear Mom,

I'm in my final stages of my time here—which means I have to do all the things I should have done two months ago in the next few days. The usual story.

It was good to talk to you by phone last week—sorry I let so much time go by without communicating. Time sometimes doesn't seem to move much in the eternal grey of Lima's winter. I had my last Sunday in Gustavo's parish the day before yesterday. The people are so lovely—all say they'll miss me a lot and hope I'll be able to come again next year.

As usual, they send you a special greeting. Mothers are important people in this country. I am ready to leave Peru for now but in spite of the difficulty of life here and the incredible suffering all around, there's a mysterious link I have with this place. Why else do I keep coming back?

I hope you have a lovely day. We'll celebrate it when we next rendezvous.

Lots of love, Jim

College of the Holy Cross. 11, January 1990
Dear Dad,

    The radio is great! I've tuned in so far to Brazil, Chile, Australia, Colombia, Malaysia, Germany, Austria, France and someplace in the South Pacific. Not to mention Boston, Amherst and Worcester public radio (highbrow music).

    Hope you are both well and enjoying your skiing forays.

                  Love, Jim

            January, 1991

    It is with a sincere apology that I write to you since I know that many of you have been deeply concerned about me, unable to locate me, and perhaps feeling excluded from my life this past year. I'm sure, or at least I hope, that deep down you know that my lack of communication has had nothing to do with you but has rather been due to my personal struggles. I want to try to make amends by sharing in this brief note some of what I have been passing through the past year and a half.

About a year ago I began to work with a psychotherapist, hoping to gain insight into some long-standing psychological issues in my life. I felt I had come to a point where patterns that had seen me through 40 years would no longer suffice.

In particular I could see that to a significant degree my life had seen a pattern of denial of self accompanied by a frustrating attempt to live up to the expectations of others. In a sense the core of my self had become lost. Now I began to see my life as both my own and as a gift of God, and I could see that I must take responsibility for choices and not take my cue from others.

If you have ever been through therapy yourself, you will know that it can be both taxing and helpful. For me the process has proved very useful in the areas of personal freedom and identity. One area that I had to look at seriously was my life as a Jesuit and a priest. Though I had really begun to grow away from the Jesuit community quite some time before, it was the fundamental ways I could not really be true to myself by remaining in the Order. Accordingly, last April I decided to resign from the priesthood and leave the community. Though I am convinced that this was a good decision, it was not an easy process for me to negotiate emotionally.

One of the things that aided to the difficulty of this past year was the need to acknowledge openly my own sexual identity as a gay man and the need to understand this identity in relation to my Christian faith and my political commitments involving Latin America and the struggle of the poor for liberation. Though the Church does not at this time support the struggle of gay and lesbian people to affirm their humanity, my decision to leave the Jesuits was not based on my being gay. (The two can quite easily go together if one chooses to live out one's sexuality as a celibate.). The decision does, however, include the desire to identify more closely with the on-going struggle for freedom for sexual minorities as well as for other oppressed groups. As for my teaching of theology here at Holy Cross in Worcester, I find that the change from being a member of the clergy to claiming my position as a member of a marginalized group in the Church as well as in society at large fits well with what I teach, the theology of liberation. In a sense I have moved from the center to the margin, where faith can perhaps grow stronger, but where securing personal and social freedom remains a task to be carried out with courage.

  The darkness and trials of these days of war make me only more eager to hear from you. Please *be in touch if you would like (20 Bowdoin St. Apt. #3, Worcester, MA 01610) This is really like starting over, and your friendship means more to me than ever.*

An Introductory Dictionary of Theology and Religious Studies was edited by Orlando O. Espin and James B. Nickoloff in 2007. This is a 1521-page tome, and I am probably the only person that has read it from cover to cover. It took me a long time, but I did learn a lot.

Jim published another book: *In, Out, and About on The Hill – LGBTQIA+Alums Reflect on Life at Holy Cross, 1978-2018*

When Jim, who hated cold weather, retired, he moved to Miami saying that he would never again live where there aren't palm trees. Winters he teaches at Barry University, Miami Shores, Florida.

As professor emeritus, he teaches at Holy Cross and Santa Clara University (in Spanish) and Australia for months every summer. When Covid attacked, many of these classes are now on zoom.

Jim has organized tours in South America and the United States for the principals of all the Catholic High Schools in Australia (19 principals in all). Presently (2023) he is winding up one of these bus tours that started in New York City and traveled through Appalachia to Georgia to visit Martin Luther King's church in Atlanta, President Carter's Presidential Library and Museum, Flannery O'Connor's home and then on to Montgomery, Alabama, ending in New Orleans. He is planning a tour for them to see parts of Mexico next summer and he thought it a good idea when I suggested Korea might be their next destination.

This is an excerpt from a letter I wrote to Jim dated Feb. 2, 2003. My husband had passed away just before 2000.

Dear Jim,

Today (Ground Hogs Day) is Dad's birthday. I've sort of talked to him a lot today. Really miss his spontaneity. Bob is very nice but when we are with other people, he seldom enters the conversation—just listens.

This cold weather I've been wearing one of mom's flannel nighties—and I keep dreaming about her—always pleasant and I wake up and lay there going over the dream again.

Now, ninety-nine years old, I often dream that I'm playing golf with friends or skiing. My mind is exercising even if I'm not!

Chapter Five

The first letter we received from No. 2 Son John was the one he wrote to us in New York. He was 13 years old.

May 15, 1963

Dear Mom and Dad,

I'm writing this letter Thursday night; tomorrow is voting day. I hope I at least make the Preliminaries!!

Lots of things have happened but nothing out of the ordinary. First off ...my guppy had babies. I haven't counted them yet, but I think about twenty-five. I put her in the five-gallon tank Friday when I took the Betta (fish) to school and Tuesday she had the babies. I took the babies out of the five-gallon tank and put them in a quart jar. Next...typping. Although I spelled typing wrong on this letter I've been doing great at school!!!!!!!

I have just typed enough thirty-word papers and one extra to pass the final exam. The number of papers was 4!!

I also cheated; but keep quiet. Shush-h-h-h! Not on the final exam but I typed a paper

(30-words) for another girl in ninth grade. She's real popular!! She might get me some votes from eighth graders.

Oh well...next... the meals have finally (I hope) turned out good but the last few days they have been pretty lousy!!! Not because of the menus but because of not enough time or too much. I either cook it extremely rare. Or burn it depending on what time Jim gets home. The first time Jim and Grandpa took Keith home and I took the meal out fifteen minutes early. All I heard was how cold the meal was!!

Wednesday, I cooked shrimp without any oil. I managed to find a couple of drops of it but not enough to cook shrimp. I'll bet you think why didn't I see the full jar of oil in the shelf. Well, I found it! After I cooked the shrimp to complete transparency!!! Don't worry, it all worked out fine! I cooked the shrimp twice but they came out to a golden tan. In fact, that was the only good meal I've made yet.

When Saturday comes, if Friday ever passes I'll bake a cake. I went up to the market and got a Hershey's cocoa cake with a fluffy white frosting mix. This may seem like a strange combination, but it was pictured on the front of the cake mix box. Actually, the only reason I got the cake was because I like different types of cake (naturally).

I had a scare when my teacher gave me a "d" notice. I not only didn't sign it but ripped it up. This startled the teacher, but I explained the action, told him why I wouldn't sign it and ended up with either a "B" or high "C".

We saw Gordon Cooper go up!! Man, was that exciting!!! On the telephone today Jim asked you if you saw it too. Just at this second Grandpa called me and Jim (Jim and I) to see Cooper land on a tape. But we saw the whole thing happen just as it did. He landed sometime around 4:30 pm and I get home at about 4:28 so I had to race home to see it really happen. I made it. I knew he was going to land because on the bus on the way home the bus driver turned on the radio.

Cooper was still going around but then all of a sudden, they said he was going to land in five minutes or so. I got off the bus and saw it.

I have been doing a lot of campaigning for presidency and I'll know tomorrow whether it has been worth it? I wore a suit to campaign in today and I'll wear it again tomorrow. All we'll do tomorrow is walk up on the stage and they'll introduce us. We don't even get to say a thing.

It's Friday morning now, I'm just as nervous as ever. I'll tell in a few hours whether I've won. Keep your fingers crossed. Bye now, I've got to get to school. Take lots of pictures and send one more letter if you can.

Sincerely yours,
John Nickoloff

John did not win President of his junior high school, but he did win President of his high school student body. Jim was vice-president the year before. They were almost two years apart in age, but only a year apart in school.

One thing I approved of was the school's rule that if they were traveling by bus for a game or any other reason, they must wear a suit. The reasoning was that it was harder to "rough house" in a suit.

Also, I know that my Dad was happy that John baked a cake. He was never interested in any food except dessert. The only thing my Dad prepared was coffee and cereal. I know for a fact that he never set foot in a market in his life.

Teenager John was camp counselor at Bluff Lake in the summertime. We received this note from him:

Dear Mom and Dad,

Today was hike day. We went to Siberia Creek. I think that's the hike Tom went to. Man, there's sure enough caves. I heard a rattlesnake and got a long stick and went after it. I couldn't see where it went but when I stuck the stick in a bush, I heard its rattle increase. Not being able to see it, I backed away and left it alone!

Some of the caves went 30 feet down. We discovered where water came up from underground streams.

Yesterday, it rained and rained. My cabin had 47 leaks. I was right in the middle of archery when the rain came again. It even rained a little on the hike today. Now it's drizzling but no leaks (yet!)

I'll print up another copy for Jim. Until then,

John

John was 16 when he left a note saying he was going to prove that man could still live like a caveman. We were not to look for him and he would return in a year. He had taken $300 out of his bank account.

Our first thought was that he was living in a cave in the mountains near Bluff Lake where he had camped as a youngster. My husband and our neighbor Bob Poolman hiked all over and then Jimmy hired an Indian tracker to no avail.

The sheriff told me that most runaways return in 5 days. This was the only time in my life that I took sleeping pills because I couldn't sleep.

Exactly 5 days later, the phone rang at 7 a.m. "This is the sheriff in the Everglades. I have a boy here who says he is your son. What do you want me to do with him?" My husband said, "Put him on a non-stop plane to Los Angeles."

John had hitchhiked across the country. Before reaching the Everglades, he bought a tent, camping stuff and a big bow and arrow, thinking he could find enough wildlife to sustain him.

He got off the bus in the middle of the Everglades and discovered there was not even a dry spot to put down his sleeping bag except in the middle of the road. Mission Impossible!

My mother lived near the L.A. airport, so we picked him up. It was his sixteenth birthday, and we had a party at my Mom's house.

John maintained that he might have been successful if he had stopped in Alabama.

John graduated from the University of California at Long Beach majoring in Botany. He had a great love for orchids and raised many in a green house on our property in Sierra Madre. We owned the lot next door, so he planted all 200 feet of it in vegetables, including this giant zucchini I picked.

My dad was living with us at the time, and he took on the watering and weeding job.

John's love for orchids took him on a trip to South America to search for orchids and fern spores. He was 23 years old. This is the only letter we received from South America:

Iquitos. Sunday, Nov. 26, 1972

Happy Thanksgiving!

I missed it down here. In fact I didn't even remember it until today. It doesn't seem like anything but tropically lazy days in Iquitos. Right now, it is about 1:30 p.m. and there is not a soul on the streets. Every day during the week the stores close from 12 to 4 in the hot part of the day. On Sundays, of course, all the stores are closed and even the rats go underground.

Iquitos is a muy lindo (very pretty) town especially when you compare it to Pucallpa or Tingo Maria. The streets are paved and it is about the first time I've been on solid ground since I've been in the jungle! The city has grown largely because it is on the portion of the Amazon River that is navigable by ocean freighters. At Iquitos the river is probably over a hundred feet deep!

My diary is badly in need of repair, having been so busy that I have hardly had any time to write anything down. So therefore, I will send you this letter as a diary of my experiences so far and hope that you will hold on to it for me for future reference.

Monday, November 20, 1972. After the first clear night in a week at Tingo Maria, the clouds moved in again this morning at 9 a.m. and it rained for two hours. Temp. Max. 86 degrees Fahrenheit Min. 71 degrees F.

Today Jose Loyase Torres showed me the University de Agraria de la Selva where he teaches. The University was small, containing only four buildings for instructions, a green house, homes for the professors, a small natural history museum, and a library. The library contained very few books although it did contain a partial collection of the Chicago Natural History Museum works on Peruvian flora. Most books were in English.

Jose wanted me to find out if there is any information on the Genus Pteridium in relation to the extraction of Silica in the stem. Walter, another professor who was the only one who could speak English and he offered his assistance in any way that I could be able to use the University's resources.

My good friends Ernesto Nunez de Prado and his wife (IBM technical advisor in Peru) and I spent the remaining day discussing the Peruvian culture.

Tuesday, November 21, 1972. I gave Jose my specimens and spores to be sent back to Los Angeles. I gave some small orchids and a bromeliad and the butterflies to Ernesto for them to take back to Lima. I packed my gear and Ernesto drove me to the bus station.

Rain at night from 12 to 8 a.m. Temp. 80 degrees Max. 68 degrees Min. After returning to Jose's to pick up my camera that I had forgotten, I walked back to the station and boarded a bus for Pucallpa.

My bus trip from Tingo Maria to Pucallpa was probably the most amazing trip I have ever taken in my life. The bus leaves late in the day because on most of the road they are working on it and so it is only open from 6 p.m. to 6 a.m. Can you believe that? Well, it's true and what is even more amazing is that they actually call it a road.

Between the two cities is one of the wettest spots in all of South America. It rains possibly five hundred inches a year, over 5 inches a day during the rainy season; and this is the rainy season! The bus was packed when we started, but that didn't stop the bus driver from picking up another twenty people along the road.

By nightfall we reached the beginning of the wet road. We waited there an hour and then the bus started the motor, and we were ready to go.

However, the trucks in front of us by this time, had sunk in the mud.

I didn't speak much Spanish and nobody on the bus spoke English so it was pretty hard to figure out what was going on. Through all the commotion, I realized that the driver wanted us to evacuate the bus while he tried to negotiate a maneuver around the trucks along the edge of this cliff.

An old lady, apparently exhausted from the trip so far, and a couple of adventurous individuals stayed in the bus while the rest of us hopped out. We didn't go far though and instead, promptly sank into the mud about three feet. Everybody was screaming and yelling and it was dark and raining. What a mess. I went over to rescue a lady who had sunk up to her waist in mud. At one time she had had very nice stockings and white heeled shoes.

But now she just looked red from shoulder to feet with reddish tropical guck.

Eventually we all realized we couldn't go around the trucks by going up the hill because the soil was entirely too soft so we sloshed along the road in the mud and only sank a foot or two. We finally made it to the bus which by this time, by some miracle, had made it past the trucks. The few who had stayed on the bus laughed and jeered at us as we slopped around in the mud, but it looked to me like they had a few grey hairs themselves.

Everybody breathed a sigh of relief as they got on the bus and everybody became a little more friendly though a lot dirtier.

We went maybe five or ten more minutes and came to a landslide over the road. Some of the truckers had been clearing it away and, in an hour, or so we were back on the road again. The overgrown, potholed muddy road (the only link the interior has with the civilized world) is amazingly narrow for allowing two-way traffic. Usually, the trucks stop while we carefully maneuver around them or vice versa. We proceeded most of the trip at about five miles an hour but occasionally, under exceptionally good conditions, we went ten m.p.h.

After six hours (50 miles) we stopped to eat at this dive. Fortunately (or unfortunately) the place was out of food so we got back on the bus and continued creeping for another three hours on into the night.

We finally stopped on the top of this mountain in fog and clouds at another place to eat (I really couldn't call it a restaurant in good conscience). We ate what mountain people eat boiled bananas (very similar to hard bread) and soup with a little rice on the side. The soup had a big animal foot in it and I wasn't sure whether it was a lizard foot or some kind of bird. It turned out to be a bird foot. I suppose it tasted okay if you like feet. However, I began the trip with a pretty bad case of the stomach cramps, and that time nothing looked good including the feet. So I had tea and we left the fog forest.

We made it into Pucallpa at six in the morning, fifteen hours later (150 miles total from Tingo Maria to Pucallpa,) and on time! They only run these trips about twice a week and in a couple of weeks, there won't be any road left due to the mucho Lluvia (big rains).

Wednesday, November 22, 1972. After the trip I was somewhat hot, tired and dazed, a little sick and in desperate need of a place to crash. I thought I would stay in a hotel for a day and then go to Iquitos but they were both full so I just sat along the curb half asleep. Then I spotted Ramon Ferrera (Natural History Museum director in Lima) breathed a sigh of relief and went off with him to have breakfast.

He said he was off to Iquitos by plane later that day and since I didn't particularly like Pucallpa at the moment, I thought it might be a pretty good place to go. I went down to the airopuerto, but the plane was full and I didn't have a reservation so I dejectedly took a taxi back to town. By this time a hotel had a room (I use the term loosely) so I just closed my eyes went into the room and fell asleep until the next day.

Thursday, November 23, 1972. I woke up though I kept my eyes closed until I got outside the hotel and wandered around the town. I went by to see Jose Pickling (Ministerio de Comerecio y Industria) his name I got from a friend in Lima. We chatted a little while about the future of Pucallpa and I derived from the conversation that there isn't much hope. There are not any paved streets, not much industry, the people don't do much, and it doesn't have anything a tourist would want. Pucallpa does have a lot of foul smells, a lot of garbage, quite a few rats and these giant vultures that comb the streets in the early mornings.

I met these pilots that fly cattle in from Brazil that have been waiting 6 days for gasoline to come in on the muddy road from Lima and by this time were pretty bored. We decided to go to Yaria Colcher (which is a name of a village not a person) where the Institute of Linguistics is located about 7 kilometers outside of Pucallpa.

We drove up there and took a boat out on this lake to the Institute. There were a lot of Americans there of all ages. The Institute has been there for 25 years trying to translate Indian languages in the Jungles. I went swimming in the lake and had a good time. In the lake are dolphins and piranhas and all kinds of other fish. The piranhas don't generally attack a person unless he sits still, so you just have to keep moving.

The natives don't like the dolphins because they are supposed to be bad. They (the dolphins) according to Indian legend come into villages at night and rape the women. During the day the men swim in the lake but the women will only go out in a canoe and bathe by splashing water on themselves. The women always face shore so that the dolphins won't cast a spell on them which in the process makes them pregnant. The weather was hot with occasional sprinkles in the afternoon.

Friday, November 24, 1972. I packed up and left Iquitos via a jet. I was going to take a boat up the river, but the only one I could find took fourteen days and probably fourteen hundred stops.

I wanted to get as far away from Pucallpa as possible, so I flew.

As I said earlier, Iquitos is very nice. I met a lot of American, Australian, and New Zealand oil riggers. I have been staying with Enrico, (don't know his last name) an electrical engineer who works on finding areas suitable for drilling. He is a Texan and has been living in and around Iquitos for two years.

He knew a man who handles expeditions into the jungle and I met him today. We arranged for a boat and an Indian guide for me for a week. At that time, I would have presumably found a spot that is suitable for my base camp.

The man's name is Moises Torres Viena and his official guide number is 91. This is not the name of the Indian but the name of the man for whom he works. Moises has an office in Iquitos

.... Jiron Lima 410-414 (office) Address Calle Brasil Home, 217, Iquitos, Peru. He does not speak much English but possibly he can take a letter to me in the bush because he often travels along that stretch of the river, at least 3 times a week.)

Well, it's off to the jungle now, you might be receiving a letter by jungle boat soon. Please write to that address when you can.

Jon
Tarzan

John changed his name legally to Jon. He was loving the cleanliness of the jungle once he got away from civilization. Fording a river, he realized it was flowing too fast for him to handle all the stuff he was carrying, so he had to let go of his backpack and all his belongings floated down the river including his antibiotics.

We heard nothing from Jon for three months. He had gotten sick, and a native found him propped against a tree. Luckily, he had left his passport and airline ticket to Florida at a village.

He arrived in Florida with only what he was wearing. Our friends, the Simons, who had lived in Sierra Madre and had moved to Florida because Mr.

Simons was an entomologist and there are more bugs in Florida, picked him up at the airport.

Mrs. Simons told me she didn't want me to see Jon until she fattened him up (he weighed only 100 lbs.) and he was a big man.

About this time, the first computer was developed, and Jon was fascinated with the concept. The first thing he did was create a chess game on the computer and soon he was working for a computer company setting up paperless systems for banks from San Francisco to New York.

John's beautiful brain was destroyed by cancer when he was 64 years old.

Chapter Six

No. 3 son Tom's first letter was written to us in New York City. He was seven years old. He made a copy of it for a school assignment.

May 16, 1963

Dear Mom and Dad,

    I hope you are having a fun time. We all wish we could go with you lucky dogs to New York.

    When you called us, it sounded like you were across the street. I wish I could go with you. I always wished I could go on the top of the Empire State Building. Our team is going to play a baseball game against the Mounties on Saturday. Our team beat them the last time we played them. Well, I think that's all I could tell you.

    Good bye,
Tom

Tom was invited to spend Christmas vacation in Hawaii with his aunt and uncle and cousin Jamie. The last day of school, he fell from a high bar and broke his arm, but that didn't stop him from going to Hawaii. He sent us a post card picture of a Hukilau and wrote:

> *Family: I'm sorry I haven't written sooner. I had a good flight over and so far I'm having a great time. I tried out a plastic bag on my cast and it worked. (written by Jamie)*

Tom sent another postcard of girls on Waikiki Beach to his brother Jim:

> *Jim: How's the snow in Sierra Madre? It was a cool 83 here today. Me and Jamie are making a movie called The Endless Winter (original). We go around the island taking pictures of good lookin' females. Wow, have we got some fantastic shots! Like the ones on the front of this card. We got your letter yesterday. Thanks! Well, I'm going to bed now. Take it easy, Tom*
>
> *(written by Jamie)*

Tom and his cousin Jamie went to a boys' camp in Santa Barbara one summer, hence this letter postmarked Santa Barbara, July 13, 1965:

Dear Mom and Dad, and the other ones that can read:

I can't believe that letter you wrote to me. I hope Tony doesn't play with little red things anymore. And I'm glad John's team won. Oh, sorry John! Way to be Brother!

Anyway, it's been freezing in the morning, and we have swimming first. After that Jamie and I go to track. In track we are running, high jumping, shot putting, and the triple jump. After track we go to baseball. After baseball we hop on the bus and go eat. After eating we go back to wrestling, basketball or gymnastics. After that we go to games. In games we play football. After football we go back on the bus to the dorms. And then we eat. After eating we usually play a game of whiffle ball. After that we have two sport films. Last Sunday we had a film called the Jackie Robinson Story. After the film we go to bed. I am looking forward to seeing you next week.

Love, Tom

Your Son of course

Tom's fascination with Hawaii led him to get jobs during his last year of high school to earn money to go back to Hawaii. He was "delivery boy" for our pharmacist neighbor, Wes Anderson and he was a waiter in an Italian restaurant.

His first letter from Hawaii:

Sunday morning. June 24, 1972

Howzit---

Everything's been going really well so far. I've been staying with Paul at his brother Mike's house. It's a real nice house in the Haleiwa on the North Shore. I've been paying for food etc. and believe it or not, here in Haleiwa, the prices are the same as they are there. Today I'm going to see about a house across the street from Pipeline. I saw an ad up at the market last night for a "male" --$120 Mo. in an outrageous 4-bedroom house with 3 other guys. Mabe it'll come through. Mike says there'll be plenty of openings at this new hotel they're building just down the road towards Honolulu about 5-8 miles from here. It should be done in a month or two. Until then, mabe I can get an odd job somewhere. A lot of people have been coming over to Mike's house this last week and all of them are really friendly.

This one guy (38 yr. old Hawaiian) who's name is Tommy also is going to see about getting me a horse. That's right.... a horse. I can't think of anywhere else in the world I'd rather have a horse than here in Hawaii. He says it'll cost me about $70-$80 to buy it and $10 a month to keep it at this ranch he owns on the northwest corner of the Island. And food and everything else for it won't cost me a cent.

But we made an agreement that if I get it (and it looks pretty good right now) I'll have to go on roundups with him. Tommy also owns land on all the islands except Kawai and commutes in his private "Cessna twin 310". Can you believe that! Yesterday me, Mike and Paul (sorry about the English Mom) went with Tommy to pick various kinds of fruit (mangos, guavas, papaia, passion fruit, etc. on his plantation up by the ranch. It was really fun.

We've been going to the north shore beaches every day this week. The last couple days the waves have been good (4-6 ft). The first few days this week we went skin diving at various places along the north shore including Waimea Bay where in the winter the waves get bigger than anywhere in the world (20-30 feet). The water is unbelievably clear and 75 degrees cold. We went skin diving just as the sun set and it was so warm, I could of stayed in all night. The fish are also beautiful to look at but almost impossible to spear with these guns Mike has, although I keep trying.

The air temp has been in the low 80's all week and perfectly clear except for the clouds and a little rain every now and then. Our house where I'm staying now is overlooking miles and miles of sugar cane fields which gives the air a most pleasant smell. I really love everything so far and I just hope it keeps going well.

I can just picture you reading this letter to Mrs. Poolman some morning next week so... Hi Mrs. Poolman... How's the war been going, I haven't heard a thing about it since I left. Don't forget to vote for tricky dick and may all your wishes come true.

Anyway, aloha for now.
Tom

Rosemary Poolman lived across the street. She would come over about 10 a.m. for a cup of coffee every morning. We would solve all the world's problems and then she would go home. Another letter from Tom:

Monday night July 3, 1972

Aloha!

Thought I'd drop a line while I have nothing to do for the moment on the eve of our "Great Independence Day." Everything is continuing to go very well; and when I say that, I mean more like fantastic. If this writing gets a little wavy, it's because I'm writing this on my new waterbed. Not brand new; it was a gift from Steve who you'll find out about shortly.

Do you remember that house I was going to "find out" about that was on the beach at Pipeline. Well, as unbelievable as it seems to me, I am now a resident there. It's a beautiful 2 story completely furnished house on the beach. If you were to look on a map of Oahu, it would be just east of Waimea Bay about 3 miles. I'm living here with 2 couples, and one other guy. We all have our own bedrooms. Mine, overlooking the mountains out the front which are the greenest in the world for all I care.

Our front yard has papaya, banana and various other flowered plants and trees, all of which I can easily go out and pick anytime. The back part of the house has a balcony that runs the full distance across the back of the house. This is overlooking our back yard of grass which is about 30 feet from house to beach.

Along the beach and grass border there are 5 giant cocoanut trees complete with cocoanuts. It's an unbelievable view from the balcony and just to add to the touch, the sun goes down almost directly in the middle of the ocean every night of the year. And the sun sets are breath-taking every night which you can imagine I'm sure.

The whole thing is a fantasy to me except when it comes to paying the bills every month. My rent is $130, which is ¼ the total, and you can figure that out yourself. It's just an unbelievable house worth $150,000 according to our real estate lady who dropped in on us the other night. The girls have been cooking the food (mostly dinners) and also handling the washing, etc. We have our own washer-dryer set up by the way which is nice.

We also have living with us 3 dogs all from the same batch, and two cats who eat the rats outside. We've been doing things all as a family which is so nice for me, the newcomer to the islands.

According to Butch and Steve (both of whom have their girlfriends here) and Brian, the North Shore or the (country) which it is often referred to as the place to be on Oahu. There are no stop signs, signals, or all the tourists that you find on the Southern part of the islands. Just open country sprinkled by small mountains, sugar and pineapple fields and just a lot of green things, etc. everywhere you look.

  Paul and I (Paul's leaving in a week or so) have been doing all kinds of fun things together this last week like cliff diving from the beautiful Waimea Falls which is really pretty insane. The rocks that you jump off, dive if you're brave enough, are 30, 40, 50 and 75 feet high. Paul and Joe (Paul's other brother here) talked me into going from the top which was crazy but I did it. You jump into a pool at the bottom of the falls, which hasn't been measured to the bottom 'cause of its depths. It's really fun once you get used to it. The water is warm, but not compared to the 78 degrees of the ocean.

  We've also done lots of skin diving and little body surfing as the waves haven't been real good as of late. But there's always things to do. Paul and I went to the Jethro Tull (Jac will know who they are) concert Saturday nite. It was really good and was sold out a couple days in advance. Steve went into town and got me the tickets.

Dad will be interested to know that Steve also has a small plane license (like himself) and promised me he'd take me to some other islands soon. He says he usually rents a Cessna, possibly a 1700 or 180 if I remember right. There's also skydiving at this airport which is about 7-8 miles from here going northwest towards the top corner of the island. Mabe if I get rich soon, I'll take that sport up. (Pardon the pun) **(He did!)**

Tomorrow I'm helping some organization that's sponsoring a 4th of July Hawaiian Independence Day celebration just down the road a few miles. I'm going to sell food tickets and mabe other odd jobs. Brian and Agnes who is my land lady (I'll probably be referring to her as Aggy in the future) got me into doing it and it will probably be fun.

I've already met a really nice girl at the meeting we had today. I've also been meeting people through the people I live with all of whom have been real nice and a few know me by name now and come over and we talk about things. I went to a party with Paul the other night before the concert that Brian and Butch took us to which was fun.

I really can't think of much else to say except that I've taken care of almost everything I've set out to do including my bank account and checking account. I haven't cashed Dad's $100 check yet though because I forgot about it until yesterday when I was putting things away. I'll do that soon. We're also getting a phone hooked up tomorrow so you can call me if you want. I'll give you the number next time.

Also, Mom, could you do me a favor by calling this girl's house and finding out her address for me because I told her I'd be writing right away. She was pretty much in the picture before I left and hopefully, she might come over this summer. Both her and her mother are really nice and all you have to say is Tom Nickoloff forgot Janet's address and only has her phone number and would like to mail some letters. I'd be much appreciative if you would do this for me, and could you send it soon.

Janet McKeehan
792-7551

So anyway, that's about it from here. Love,
Tom

The people living with me, animals included:
Steve & Sandy
Butch & Kathy

Me
Brian

Lug-nut.)
Budweiser (dogs
Ralph)

Konin) cats
Zac)

And also a fish tank full of fish.

(Between this letter and the next, Tom had moved to Kauai to attend college.)

July 17, 1972

Greetings everybody,
 Not a whole lot of changes from this end. I have to admit there are a few things new though. I met this really nice Vietnamese (sp?) girl at school a week or so ago and she and I have just about covered the whole island in her car. Actually, she isn't Vietnamese, she just looks that way. Pamela is ½ Chinese, half Japanese. Very intelligent, more so than me in a lot of ways but that's life on a small island. We get along very well together and so far,

I've gotten to see a lot of what Kauai is all about. She used to live here before she moved to Washington State and in between that she's been all around the world. Her favorite spot is India. Why? She says the people there lead very simple and sometimes struggling lives on the outside, but on the inside, their minds are much more complete and higher than the Americans could ever be. No drugs needed (alcohol, stimulants, tranquilizers, pot, etc.) or psychedelics or just any of a thousand different things that we Americans depend on every day. What could I say, except that I'm still glad I'm an American, although I'd like to go see a lot of these different cultures, too, and form "my" opinion.

But, anyway, back to Kawai: this island is just one beautiful place altogether like the other islands. Kawai has many different geographical features. An almost dry desert-like north-west corner here is where the famous Little Grand Canyon of the Pacific lies. I only got to see a small part of it from the main highway this time, but I'll go see the whole thing someday. On the way up there along the west side of the island are small towns here and there and mostly sugar cane. Beautiful beaches all along the way. Farther down on the southern coast are small bays and towns. There is where I'd like to live.

Hanapepe is a beautiful town spread out from the ocean up this valley and along the ridges. I almost got a house there, but someone beat me to it. There are quite a few houses for rent now and then around that area. Mabe I'll get lucky pretty soon so I could move out there.

Last Sunday we drove up the eastern (Lihue) side of the island. Just as beautiful as the other. This time we drove past the Wailea River and on up lots of sugar cane fields that go all the way up to the foot of Mt. Waialae, highest mountain on the island. The top is the wettest spot on the earth. We drove all the way to Hanalei Bay and farther to the Na Pali Coast. There's no road that connects that northern most corner of the island, but there is a trail that goes along the cliffs that drop off to ocean far below. Unbelievable sight! There are no words to describe this hike—you just have to take it someday and see for yourself.

If you stay on this trail, it will take you eventually to Kalalau Valley. This valley (we didn't make the hike; it would take a week to do the whole adventure: something to look forward to!) but as I was saying, this valley is inaccessible by land; at some parts you have to swim around these cliffs to stay on this trail!

I hear the valley itself is just fantastically beautiful in all respects. There are other valleys farther back, too (the Valley of the Lost Tribes). It would take months to explore all these spots. I who have seen it: a truly unforgettable place. Kauai—yes!

O.K. now, what else...... Oh yes—school. (as if I forgot) School has been, well let's say it has been another interesting experience. I like my classes and even more I like my teachers. I am learning much. My Hawaiian history teacher is great. Reminds me of Mr. Sutro—young, full of new ideas and information. We're s'pose to go on some interesting field trips soon. He's not Hawaiian at all—definitely "haole" (white man) like most of the students in our class. Our classes are mostly small except my zoology class.

The school itself is not really that well-off; compared, that is, to the Oahu University campus. We have no cafeteria, and 1 counselor for all 1,000 students. The campus itself is very poorly kept up. I have yet to see anybody (janitor, gardener, etc.) cleaning up or doing anything around the grounds. It just doesn't look very good at all. As a matter of fact, it's terrible! But I can live with that, because the campus is probably the only spot on Kauai that's like that.

The rest of my time is spent on practicing the guitar or lazing around the park or playing in the ocean across the street. Also have taken up fishing but I have yet to catch one of these damn things. A lot of bites though.

Not much else; things are looking better though. I just wish I could move into a house with a few things like an ice box and stove for starters.

When are you coming to Hawaii? And do you think you could ship or mabe bring my box of records over here—also my bedspread. Debbie Anderson should be coming over real soon—like mabe next week or thereafter. Mabe she can bring the bed spread.

That's all for now, see ya,

Love, Tom

(Debbie, our neighbor in Sierra Madre, is married and lives on the island of Maui selling real estate.)

This next letter was written before Tom moved to Kauai:

August 12, 1972

Grandma Mimi and Grandpa Jim,

    Sorry I haven't written earlier, but time has been going by so fast I can't believe it. You've probably heard that I've moved into a house already and now I feel like the coming and settling down part of my trip is over with. I am really happy with everything so far; the people I live with are so nice to me. That they make me feel really at home already. I have a little part time job working with one of the guys I'm living with, and I hope to find a better job soon. So far though I've been more or less on a vacation than anything.

    The North Shore is the coolest spot on Oahu as we get the wind and breezes in the mornings and evenings. This makes the climate here nice at all times and I really feel healthier just living here. Our house is right on the beach and from our balcony, we can watch the sun set every night which is so beautiful, it makes me feel happy and satisfied inside. After watching it go down, I can reflect on what I've been doing so far and what lies ahead for me while living here in Hawaii.

    As for the things we've been doing, skin diving has been the most fun. Also, one of the guys here (Steve) has a pilot's license and took me and

2 other friends flying around the island last week. From a small plane you can really see where everything is located. We flew right over Uncle Newel's house in Kaneohe, but I didn't see anyone. I hear that most of the Bohnetts are on the mainland at this time. I also heard that you (Grandma) were in the hospital with a leg ailment, and I hope you feel better now and that it's been over and done with.

My love to both you and Grandpa and hope to hear from you soon if possible. Love, Tom

On the back of the envelope, in Grandma Mimi's handwriting, were notes she must have taken regarding an upcoming trip to Europe:

> Flight Europe 10:30 P.M.
> Arrive Monday 6:55 Frankfort. Stay overnight
> From Frankfort Ljubljana

Ljubljana was Grandma Mimi's birthplace in Slovenia. When she was born, Franz Joseph was her King as Slovenia was part of Austria.

Another letter from Tom from Oahu:

August 15, 1972

Hello--

    Not a whole lot to say, but there hasn't been any problems. I'm hoping to work at this ritzy hotel in Kahuku down the road. I'll find out in the next couple days. I've been staying with Butch at his old house with his friends in Pacific Heights which is up on the mountain over-looking Honolulu. There's been a south swell from some hurricanes close to here and the waves have been unreal;' 8-10 feet at Sandi Beach which is close to the Blow Hole.

    It's too long a drive from the country everyday so we're staying at this house in P.H. for a few days until the swell goes down. There's not too much surf on the North Shore during the summer these days. I had a collision with the bottom last week at Pipeline body surfing. The coral cut my shoulder and above my eye but nothing serious. It was fun.

    I got a letter from Jim yesterday. He told me Chris is coming to Hawaii the end of this week. He gave me a phone number to reach her. I'll get her to come up to the house for a day or so this weekend. It should be worth a few laughs. Butch and I have been making candles this last week.

We're hoping to sell some at this rock-festival in two weeks at the Crater. We bought as an investment 55 lbs. of candle wax yesterday for $15. It's a lot of fun if nothing else just to make them. I'm going to see "big-timer" Leon Russel this weekend also. Ask Jac who he is, he'll tell you. It should be a good concert. Sorry I'm not in any of the pictures, but I have some more I took with an "instamatic," but they haven't been developed yet. There's nowhere on the North Shore that will do it, so it'll just have to wait.

    Tom Hamilton Jr. played in an all-star football game here Saturday. California all-stars against Hawaiian all-stars. They ran an article in the paper about him and his team (Pasadena) last week before the game. I didn't go to their game though. Tom threw a touchdown pass and we won 20-0. I heard it was a good game. Until my next letter, Good-by, love and kisses, and farewell,

    Tom

    October 24, 1972

    Hello Everyone,

    I'm back safe and sound. Nothing's changed here except the beach out front of our house. It's about ½ as big now since we had our first big waves this winter last week. It was really exciting. We got the report of "large" swells to hit the North Shore the night before. When we woke up the next morning, I saw them! The first wave I saw break looked to me about 30 feet tall. I've never seen anything more spectacular than these waves. At Pipeline there were about 5 guys out surfing—big name dudes. You'd just have to see them surf to believe it. They're just fantastic.

It stayed big all day and there were quite a few surfers going out off and on all day. I went out body surfing that afternoon and caught only one wave--probably about an 8-foot wave and really got a nice ride. But that was all I did that day--most of the time I was just trying to stay alive.

Jim Dancy wouldn't go out at all. But he went out the next day, but didn't ride anything. He's still afraid, but I don't blame him at all. I was shook up a couple of times, too. The helicopters were picking guys up out of the water at sunset down the road who had wiped out badly.

These last couple of weeks have been a consistent 6 feet all day. I bought a surfboard for $10 from Blake and I'm slowly but surely getting better. I'm also working five days a week. Mon, Tues, 3 p.m. to 11 p.m. Fri, Sat, Sun, 5 to 11 p.m.

It's nice because I have most of the day off before I go. But it's still hard to get there on time hitchhiking, but I've had pretty good luck so far. By the way, (as if I wasn't leading up to it) Dad, do you still ride the bike or could you let me use it over here—it would be great to ride to work.

    I'm pretty sure Jim Dancy's going home at the end of this month. We've really had a lot of fun. Last night we went to the show in Haleiwa with Sid and Mike Hardy. Saw the "Graduate" and "Goodbye, Columbus." I'd seen the Graduate before but didn't remember anything. They were both great. And for a dollar-you can't beat that.

    Babes--(brother Tony) How's football? I hear you're playing middle guard and defensive captain? It seems like yesterday I was playing Pop Warner. I watched one of the teams from Wialua work out the other day. I think they were midjets. They really looked good. You wouldn't have any problem losing weight over here--humidity about 70% and temp. about 85 degrees. Fun eh?

    John--Drop me a line from Peru when you get down there so I'll know where you are and we can keep in touch.

Jac—How's Pasadena High School? Are you and Will Wilburn still cruzing the campus?

Well, the waves are calling for me so surf's up.

Love, Tom

October 24, 1972

Hello Hello—Time has just been flying by lately. As they would say here in Hawaii—"easy". Thank you for the camera but I haven't been taking any pictures yet. But soon the time will come. I got the job I was telling you about before. At the Kuilima Hotel. The same place President Nixon and the Japanese delegation stayed for 3 days about a week ago. You should have seen the security for that man—unbelievable. He rented the two top floors (192 rooms) and every employee and guest got checked every time you entered or left the hotel.

About the hotel—by far the plushest, biggest and most expensive on the island. It was just built last year by Del Web (Thunderbird, Sahara, Mint, etc.) and cost him 50 million dollars. It's located 75 miles down the road from Pipeline; right on a point and is surrounded on 3 sides by the ocean. The only hotel on the Northern half of the island.

I work from 2 p.m. to 10 p.m. 5 days a week as a member of the banquet-set-up crew. It usually takes me about an hour to set up chairs and tables and then the next 7 hours is taken up by watching the movies they show every night or eating, drinking or just plain sleeping. It's quite a cruising job if I say so myself. I clear $3.00 hr. easily and sometimes from tips etc. I make almost $4 an hour. You should see me in my "Aloha" shirt—pretty casual. (Tom was 18 so not old enough to serve liquor to the guests.)

They have professional dancing and comedy acts every day and night, and free hula lessons every morning. All in all, I'm very happy with the job so far.

I think Jim and Mike are going back soon. They both want to go back and work. There's no jobs on the North Shore for them. It would take at least 2 months for them to get a job at the hotel. But, while they have been here, we've been having more than our share of fun. The last couple days the waves here have been 6-8 feet all day. That's pretty hairy for me but I'm getting used to it now. I had a chance to go to Kauai for 3 months and live off the land in some valleys that are supposed to be some of the most beautiful spots in the world. But I'm going to work and stay here instead, at least thru the winter.

(These two friends are still on Tom's cell phone text list).

How are things in Sierra Madre? The Olympic tragedy was unreal. When will people stop fighting and get their shit together? Probably never. I haven't watched T.V. or listened to radio since I've been here. It's a very nice change. See you whenever,

Love & kisses, Tom

P.S. I hear Hershel Ramsey is the middle linebacker for U.C.L.A. this year--unreal. U.S.C. over Arkansas—maybe undefeated?

Brother Jim wrote to Tom from Andong, Korea dated 8 March 1973:

Hey there, Cook!

Just a few minutes until lunch, so I thought I'd sit down and pen you a few birthday lines. I've figured out why I. was so lazy in Hawaii, so reluctant to help you with the food, I mean, you see, here in Korea I'm waited on like a king—never lift a finger for anything "domestic" like cooking, washing, cleaning, etc. so I guess I just slipped into my 'Korean routine' while I was staying at Pipeline. I wonder what I'll be like after another year of this life!

So here it is mid-March already (by the time you get this) and time for your B-Day—19, well I can't say that's one of the "biggies" —you got almost all your rights at 18—but anyway it's an occasion for a celebration, and I hope yours is happy.

For my part, I've been doing a little celebrating too—several of my close friends here are preparing to leave after their 2-year service, and we've been wining and dining them on their way out. The whole process gives rise to that old feeling of "Where are they going? and "Where am I going? and "Will we ever see each other again?

It's been good to be together, but it seems that a parting always comes, and then you wonder what the whole thing was about if this is the final result of two years of friendship. Anyway, enough of this sentimentality!

So, have you got a job yet? I don't, amazingly enough. In typical Korean (I take no blame, you notice) fashion, my job is completely disorganized, and I can see that it'll take weeks before things are moving smoothly—if ever.

I have to go up to Seoul again tomorrow for a few days. I can already see that I'll be getting in my share of the train and bus role plays.

Well, this is just a short note to let you know that today's bright sun shines from here to there—across the countless waves of the blue Ocean and that where minds are joined, so are spirits.

I hope the Good Spirit fills "your day" on March 16!

Your brother and friend,
Jim

P.S. Greetings to all! And to Jac "Hey man, like what's up?"

By September 1973, Tom had decided to go to college on the island of Kauai.

Sunday night   Sept. 2, 1973

Well, hello everybody,

It's been a very weird start for me this time. I've had a lot of bad luck and also a lot of very good luck, so what can I say.

It all started back on Oahu when. I first got there. I stayed the 1st night at the Holiday Inn at the airport. The next day (Tues) I set out to find some sort of transportation to take to Kauai. I couldn't find anything at first (I was mainly looking for cheap cars) but there was really nothing that was in my range. So, I thought about a motorcycle.

  Well, I finally found one that this dude was selling (B.S.A.). So, I went out there to Barbers Point and looked at it and drove it around and ended up buying it and filling out all the legal papers and so on and so forth. Well, that same day (Tues still), I went over to Butch's house in Kaneohe to stay a day and night there with him and Leigh. So, I did and decided to go down to the D.M.V. to register my new bike the next day.

  This was Wed. now. I was on my way to Honolulu when I pulled into a gas station for some gas and when I went to kick the bike over, it felt as though there were no gears left in the gear box. I was to find out in a matter of minutes that the gear box was shot! Of all the bad luck!! The second day after I bought it!

  Well, I got a ride back to Butch's and we went down and picked it up in a friend's truck that night. I was planning on flying it over to Kauai the next day. So now I was really on the spot. I called up this B.S.A. dealer in town and they say they'll fix it but not for at least a couple of weeks!

I knew I had to get over to Kauai before Friday afternoon so I could register for school before it was too late. When I got there, I found out my plane wasn't going to leave until 8:05 that night. That's great, I said to myself; now I'll be flying into a place I've never been in pitch black surroundings!

When I got there, I was right, I couldn't see anything at all, so I called for a taxi to take me to the nearest hotel. He took me to the Kauai Surf which I was to find out the rates here are only 24 dollars a night. Well, I "freaked" of course and turned around and left. I got a taxi driver to take me to a cheaper (much cheaper) place. He did and I slept at the Hana Malu Motel for $8.50 that night.

I woke up the next morning and looked outside and it was beautiful! But I didn't have the faintest idea where I was either. I didn't even know if I was in Lihue. I found out I was about 5 miles out of town, so I took off (with suitcase, bags of junk, and my guitar) walking down this road that no cars were even on.

I finally did get a ride by this guy and asked him where the school was, and he said he'd take me.

I was joyful to say the least. So, I got to school and it looked pretty good until I found out they were classifying me as a non-resident. Well, I blew-up at this and I went outside and tried to decide what to do now. Went back in and talked to this mean (and I mean mean) Hawaiian man.

I told him I was a resident because of this and that and that I couldn't come close to the $300 non-resident fee now, so he answered my prayer and said O.K. you're a resident.

I took off after paying $25 tuition, for the town of Lihue. I found a newspaper and started looking for somewhere to stay. I knew it couldn't be very far from school since now I didn't have my transportation to get there and back. Would you believe nothing on the whole island?! So, I stayed at the motel the next two nights.

I woke up this morning and saw this hotel-apt. that was pretty close to school (walking distance) and asked if he had any rooms for rent and what do you know, he did! So, I check in here. I also saw a couple of houses for rent in this afternoon's paper, but they are much too far from school, about 10 to 15 miles which would be great if I had my bike right now, but I don't!

What I was thinking is that when I go back for court, on my way back, the bike should be ready by then and I'll pick it up and bring it over here with me. Then I can move out of this one room apt. and move into a house with someone around the island somewhere.

This place doesn't have any cooking facilities or refrigerator, so I have to eat dry food or go down to the local coffee shop to eat. It's gotten to be very expensive to do it that way. Which brings me to where I am right now--"broke". I have just a few dollars left from these problems and I'm going to need some money to pay for my books right away. I'm paid here at the apartment through the 1st half of this month but not the second. It's $160 a month. I think a hundred and twenty-five would get me through this month. They do have work for students at the school, so mabe by next month I could work and cover the extra costs and move out as soon as possible into a house. I understand Debbie Anderson is coming over; so she can help share the bills. Anyway, could you send the money as soon as possible please. Thanks.

I'm all registered and ready to start tomorrow. My classes should be interesting.

Algebra-trig, Social Science, Hawaiian History. They shouldn't be too bad. I think I'm ready now, so we'll see real soon.

That's it for now, I'll keep in touch.

Love, Tom

My address: Tom Nickoloff c/o
Ocean View Motel
R.R. 1 Box 192
Nawiliwili Kauai, H.I.
96766

October 16, 1973

Dad and Bros.,

Just a short note, this time.

I found a house! Yep—I sure did. It's small and I share the rent with a school bud. It cost us $400 a month so we split it and it works out great. It's furnished with all the necessary things and there's no utility charge. It's situated in a beautiful little valley with cows and pasture all around and other small houses. We're actually in a group of small houses (4 or 5). I can also still walk to school cause it's not far. Neither of us have cars so it works out perfect. I guess if you're coming over with Mom, then you'll see everything for yourself. Anyway, my new address is:

Tom Nickoloff

R.R. 1. 174

Lihue, Ka., Hi. 96766

Also, could you bring my bedspread and photo album of Hawaii. I need both. Also, if you could bring my current ski and soaring issues, that would be great! Thanks, Dad.... Tom

This next letter was addressed to me:

June 25, 1974

First, thanks Mom for the letter and the surprise that was inside. I was sorry to hear about Grandpa Tanny. Hope he and Grandma are getting better now.

As for me, here is the story:

My house that I'm living in with Mark and Steve is pretty all right. Problem is there's no furniture in this one but we're getting a few odds and ends here and there already.

The distance from school is about 13 miles which is pretty far. I sold my motorcycle about 2

weeks ago for $500. The reason or should I say reasons are pretty good ones:
    1--too many problems with carburetor.
    2--a chance to sell it for what it cost me.
    3--I needed some denero!

Also, I had a few close calls out on the highway with crazy Kauai drivers so that was enough to make me want to live and sell the crazy thing. I've decided that if I get another motorcycle someday, it's going to be a dirt bike for off-road riding--seems a little more sane.

Right now, I get a ride in with Steve in the mornings to school and hitchhike back every day. Not bad really. You meet a lot of (and a few not so) nice people. As a matter of fact, the other day I got picked up by a great couple from Denver who were vacationing here for a week. As it turned out the man (Gill) asked me where he could stop and get a beer. I told him the Koloa Tavern was close so they invited me to come in with them and we talked about me and also about their kids back in Colorado (all ski nuts I might add) and Gill told me he owns a construction company outside of Denver.

Well, I asked him if he needed any help like mabe this summer and he said, "Sure Tom, and we could put you on if you came up." So, it looks like

I might be working in Colorado this summer if I decide to move from here.

I asked Mary (his wife) about schools up there and she told me all about them--where they are, the good ones from the bad ones. I don't know but it might be worth checking into for next year. What do you think? I was pretty jazzed to say the least about the whole idea.

The gas situation here on Kauai is incredible. The lines (with no exaggeration) here are sometimes 2 miles long and always at least ½ mile. Can you believe that? It's insane. It's also kept me from buying a car right away. So, I'll just wait and hopefully things will change in the not-so-distant future. It all depends on our congressmen here—if they can convince the federal govt. that Hawaii needs more gas than what it's getting. I heard we might try and get gas from Canada—whatever, if it works, I'm all for it. So much for gasoline.

I work for Steve at night here developing film for 3 to 4 hours a night. It works out pretty good. I make enough for rent and food etc. Tell Jac, I've probably developed more pictures in the last week than he's done in his whole photography career (approx. 120 a night) Not bad, eh? Since I knew nothing about it before. It has been one more little thing to learn; and get a little satisfaction with my work too.

Just about it for now. We'll get in touch again later. All my love and aloha, Tom

Tom took pictures of and for guests at a hotel and developed them at night and posted them at the hotel the next day.

October 21, 1974

Aloha everyone,

Fun talking to everyone on the phone. Tony sounds like an old man over the phone. Afraid to think how tall he'll be when I see him next. O.K. by me though—don't mind being short. Here in Hawaii everybody is short anyway.

I'm about at the half-way point here at K.C.C. This semester I took one midterm the other day for my Sosh class "Marriage and Family." Mostly common-sense sort of stuff. As usual I'm getting into my history class most. This time it's World Civilizations. I got my favorite teacher for the class too. Remember, Mom, the guy I told you reminded me of Sutro—it's him, Mr. Bushnell. He's really great.

Everything else is fine with school. If I do go through with my plans to go to P.C.C. next semester, is there going to be any problem getting registered? Could you find out, Mom, if I can do it at Christmas vacation.

Everything and everybody else over here is fine. Steve's still working hard as a team in the photography business. We're starting at the Kauai Resort soon. Going to be more work for us and more fun too.

Thanks again for the money, Dad.

Take care, Tom

P.S. Yes, I got the picture of the house from the air. Pretty neat you guys.

Monday, Dec. 2, 1974

Well Aloha for the last time from Hawaii. I can't believe it, but this will be my last letter to anyone probably, from here in Hawaii, that is. Do you realize I've been here for over 2 ½ years?! Doesn't really seem that long. Anyway, we got plenty of time to remember the past when I get home so about the present situation, this is what's important:

I received a letter from Mr. Steve Parry the other day; and he informs me that he's getting married on Dec. 14th. Can you believe it--Steve Parry married? Anyway, this changes my plans abruptly and as of now I will be returning about 2 weeks earlier than I thought. It's not going to be easy, but I figure I probably can get all my shit together and be home for his wedding before Sat, December 14th.

My reservations stand like this:
Pan Am flight #812
lv: Honolulu 10:45 a.m.
arr: L.A. 5:50 p.m.

10 days from today! Wow!

Hope someone can meet me at the airport Thursday evening. Until then

Aloha and take care,

Tom

Returning to Sierra Madre, Tom planned on attending Pasadena City College. Unfortunately, they said he was not a California resident so he wouldn't be able to attend without paying full tuition. This really made me mad as we have been paying California taxes forever!

With this disappointment, Tom and his best friend Marco decided to go to Steamboat, Colorado. Their plan was to take Marco's Mom's Mexican recipes and open a Mexican restaurant in Steamboat. On arrival, they discovered there was already a Mexican Restaurant named Dos Amigos in this small town.

March 8. 1975

Hello!

Another day and another way. How's every-body down there? Well, now that March is here, the place is freaking out with skiers, tourists and what-have-you. The crowded conditions on the mountain is keeping the locals off including myself and now the talk of warmer temps in Mexico and California is the word of the day.

Included here are some pictures of the area and our apt. No. 1 is taken from our balcony of the mountain and of the restaurant which is the building circled with our parking lot in the foreground.

No. 2 is a front view of Dos Amigos with the sign on the right. We seat only 60 people, but the bar area is probably bigger than the dining room (bad design). We still do 180 dinners a night which isn't bad.

This last week the temp dropped real low and freaked me out when I walked home the other night and it was 35 degrees below out. Amazing how things go on here normally at that temp. You really have to be careful about frostbite in this weather as it can get you in a matter of minutes. But amazing, still I have been cold free all winter long.

Our lease ends on the apartment in April. I think I will keep working at Dos Amigos and move outside of town this spring. You were talking about coming out. The best time is to wait until June or July because here in April, May this place turns into a mud bath and nobody enjoys it for a couple months until it dries out. So why don't you wait until then.

Adios for now,
Tom

October 1, 1075

Howzit?

Made it up here with no problems or incidents to speak of. It is exactly 1000 miles from Sierra Madre. Beautiful country here in

Colorado and also coming up through Utah. Saw B.Y.U. in Provo--real nice location beneath the mountains.

Marco has been busy checking out businesses right here in Ski Time Square. Big mouth DeSilva knows everybody in town already and he's been introducing me to them all. Mostly condos for rent, all fairly new around here, although Steamboat town looks very old with the buildings and all.

I don't think we'll be doing anything with the original Mexican joint. Talking about too much money to get it started. In our little area here in Ski Square Village beneath the mountain, there are all types of things going on. Post office, stores, small restaurants, bars, etc. and all run by young type people. Marco and I are going to see what we can do with one of them.

Happy to say my car ran "primo" all the way up here and the altitude hasn't effected it either. We're at about 7,000 feet here in town.

See ya,

Tom

November 11, 1975

Here we go—

Made it back with no problems. Very nice weather for the last week and it melted all the snow from the week before. But last night a new storm dumped another foot and its winter from here on out, looks like. They say we won't be able to see the ground till next May sometime. Hmmmm.

Anyway, we're all comfortable here in the Square.

Marco and I have been busy planning our attack on the Tugboat Inn. We sat down with 3 of the 4 men who are in business (owners) with most of the bars and restaurants in Steamboat last week and showed them our plans and it all went over really well considering neither one of us had been in this situation before.

We got dressed up and went into their downtown office with our notebooks in hand. Everything written out and in order. They were all pleased with it all---and come Monday they said we can sign the legals. We're starting with a $200 sliding sale lease that definitely will help both sides. The one big one that we didn't figure in at all was the security deposit. $3000 big ones is what they want. Marco and I took a couple of hard swallows and eventually told them no way.

But we told them mabe we could work out a $500 down and pay it as we go type of deal. Seemed O.K. to them. Anyway, I'm going to talk to you over the phone, Dad, probably before you get this letter and check a few details with yourself. See what you think.

All in all, I'm happier than hell (Marco too!). We got some great advertising tips in mind, and we got plenty of P.R. work going. Everybody in town is pulling for us which is getting me so excited I can't stand to wait till the grand opening. Oh Yea! The kid in business.

A lot of creeps around here (one in particular) that have been doing different things in the last couple of years that say we won't make it for this or that reason. Too optimistic to listen though at least to this one jerk. Apparently, he's tried all sorts of things (he's got a piece of everything here in Steamboat and still hasn't made a dime). It's just giving Marco and me a little more incentive to show him and everybody else we can.

We might be open for lunch also and expand the menu and hours too, but that's good, more the better.

Saw the movie Earthquake last night. Every big building in L.A. went down, freeways, too. Dams broke and all in all it's the biggest disaster in U.S. history. Cal Tech registered it at 9.9 on the Richter scale. Ooo-wee! Doesn't look good for the city where all my people live. Careful you folks! Most important I think, don't go see that movie.

All for now. See ya! Take care.

Tom

December 8, 1975

Me and Steamboat are coming closer and closer to getting it altogether finally. Marco and I decided to go through with the cooking job at the fine new Mexican restaurant right here by the mountain. We are the head chefs! Not bad at all. We started learning the recipes this week and the place (Dos Amigos) is going to open up next Saturday. It's a big place. Giant modern kitchen, too. We should get plenty of experience where we need it. Mabe by next year we could do something on our own. Either that or stay with these guys for a while and grow with them.

Good people to work for at any rate. Matter of fact, they told us we could travel to Vail in January and cook for a week there for fun (and ski) and their cooks would come here. They have two Mex. places that are doing well down there.

The weather took a change again. Been real clear for a week now. Snow's melting and the skiers are bummed. I did go skiing once last week and that was fun. Tee-shirt conditions and we had a ball. We're expecting storm conditions to get here in the next couple days. No matter. We're going to be concentrating on the kitchen anyway for a while. We work nights (picked the shift) as a team. They're starting us at $450 month salary and it goes up from there. Not too bad. Marco and I are starting a savings trip and plan to put away at least $50 or so a week each. By next April we'll use this for a house or job thing if we decide to stick around.

Anyway, that's it for now. I was going to call over Thanksgiving and apologize for not. To tell you the truth, we were all up at the nice condo complex feasting out and forgot all about your party that was happening and before I knew it, it was 12:00 and too late to do anything about it.

All else is well and pray that all is well with you all, too.   Take care, Tom

Tom and Mom in Steamboat

October 14, 1976

Hi Everybody:

I came up here to Steamboat last week. The town looks great and the weather even better. You just can't beat the Rockies in the summer. I'm real happy to get up here even for just two weeks. The heat and humidity in Hot 'Lanta was getting to be a drag. One more month and it will be over.

I've been chatting with my boys Jim and Bill about the future of our food up here at Dos and they both want to go with it again somewhere else. (I just read that line over to myself---not much sense.).

What I was trying to say is they want to do another one mabe down South. That's what I'm going to work on--finding the location, right building, licenses, permits, taxes, etc. If all of these requirements sound good to them, we'll go with it after Christmas. Hopefully sooner, depending on how much it'll cost.

So, it's back to Atlanta next week to start doing this. We are also looking not just at Atlanta, but mabe Athens, Ga. where the University of Georgia is located. Plenty of people there and with the college there, much of the younger clientele; the kind we like to see. It's only 40 miles from Atlanta.

Thanks for the chiles. They worked out good for me. I've been fooling around with some new stuff, getting better and better and so is Dos Amigos of Steamboat. This summer the town's population has doubled for this time of year. Lots of activities happening. Dos is "The" restaurant in town. They're doing 200+ all week (a great winter night 2 years ago). I've been working in the kitchen all week to help out. It's been fun.

Hey, if you hear anything from Tony, tell him I'll be here till the end of this month before I go back down. He can get in touch with me here at Dos Amigos. So that's pretty much the scoop. I'll keep you all posted this summer as things happen. Till then later, Tom

January 1976

Hey, hey, hey,

How's everybody down there. Had a nice Christmas here. Thank you all for the gifts. Mom, the sweater is beautiful. I love it. Got a nice letter from brother Jim the other day, too.

Here, things are well, working hard--6 days. Got a raise $625 a month. It's a nice feeling being in charge. Good possibilities too for more and the main thing is the experience. I'm learning exactly what it takes to run a full-on kitchen. Apparently, I'm doing a pretty fair job of it with the raise and all.

Bob Talbot arrived yesterday. Soon as Marco gets back, we'll be the team again.

Another note from Atlanta:

Everythings fine. Still here in Atlanta. Nobody ready to go down to Mexico so I decided to stay here until June. I talked to J.G.

and Bill in Steamboat and they are both going on vacation until next month. We're going to get together when they return either here or Steamboat. I've been checking for spots down here. They are interested in the South again. Hopefully by the end of the summer we'll be ready to do it again. I'm working as a 1 cook at this restaurant E.J.s (fancy gourmet place) learning some sauté type stuff in the meantime.

Tom met his wife Dixie working at E.J.s. They decided, "Why not open our own restaurant?". And so, La Paz was born. The first restaurant was opened in the Sandy Springs neighborhood of Atlanta and mushroomed to nine restaurants in six Southern states. Tom lost all the restaurants in the 2008 depression.

Tom has two daughters, Mary with Dixie and Camila (22) with his second wife, Erica. Daughter Mary and husband Aaron are parents of Avery James (8) and Natalie (5).

Mary helps out in a pre-school and Aaron is an engineer and works for a Japanese company that makes farm equipment. He travels a lot to Japan.

They live in Jasper, Georgia and just celebrated their tenth anniversary in Italy.

Jim, Jon, Tom, Jac, Tony

His daughter Camila is going to a beauty school as she and her mother Erika are thinking about opening a beauty salon business. I received this lovely letter from Erika:

Sunday Dec. 4, 2022

Dear Ginny,

So today is the day! The day I decided to take a moment to rest and do something I have been wanting to do: to write a letter to my sweet and wise Ginny, the only mother-in-law I ever had!

How are you doing, Ginny? How is life, writing, and living the life of Virginia Nickoloff?

I want to take the moment to recognize how thankful I am to have you in my life. With respect, love, and open arms you received me in your family and you accepted me just for being me...Erika. And I remember our times together celebrating moments in life, smiling, eating good food, listening to all your stories was mesmerizing. I could spend hours or days listening what you have to say from your coffer of memories.

Love also your love stories with Mr. James and then in the later days the times and trips shared with Mr. Bob. I loved seeing you dancing and I enjoyed having a glass (or two) of wine, your favorite white wine.

Thank you for showing me all your pictures, all your fabulous closet with great dresses through all the years, for showing me the dresses your mom made for you.

Thank you for you, your laugh, your honesty, your wisdom, to always say what it is needed to be said without making long stories.

Well, I just wanted you to know no matter if I am not visiting very often, you are always in my mind and I always said it to Tom, you are the best Tom ever had in his life and I am so happy to see how mucho you are loved by your sons and how much they care.

I want to also thank you for being a wonderful human being. You inspire me to live, to travel to see life different and even to write.

Thank you for bringing in this life Thomas and Camilla. I have experiences that brought so many great things and love.

It was very amazing seeing you accepting the Lord Jesus into your life. (Funny because He has really been with you your whole life.).

Okay, time to say bye and once again thank you for your being in my life. I love you mucho!

Your Latina daughter in law, Erika

Chapter Seven

Number 4 son Jac is what I call a positive thinker. When summer came, he told me he had a job teaching swimming at the Jewish Center. When he didn't leave the house, I asked him about it and he said, "I could have had it if I had applied." He did spend many summers at Camp Bluff Lake as a guest and as a counselor. The kids were required to write to their parents. Here is a letter Jac wrote from camp:

August 11, 1972

Hello—

It may seem like I haven't written in 1 1/2 weeks, but that's wrong. I wrote the last week but never got around to sending it. The reason is simple. I don't have time. I'm a full counselor now with my own cabin. Not only that, but I'm getting payed $40! You may think that counselors shouldn't get payed but I think they should. It's a harder job than you think. Not much else happening. Sorry I couldn't tell you I wasn't coming down last Saturday, but I didn't know either. I'm not coming back next week either so don't plan on it.

What I need is:
1. My stereo
2. Some frogs (for my snake)
3. Stamps (so I can mail you letters)
4. Money (I'm running low because the extra week. I leave the amount up to your discretion)
5. More money, again (see parenthesis #4)

I hope Sheba's all right. (our dog) Feed the cat. My campers are a bunch of smart asses. If I tell them not to throw rocks, they do it within 5 seconds. I guess I'll be coming home after next week. See ya then. Jac

P.S. Thanks for the laces.

(From camp a year later.)

June 18, 1973 To whom it may concern:

Hello, I made it up here and you might of heard from Ken what happened with John's junk, etc. Anyway, the first day is over and I'm head man in charge of archery. Great, eh? I finally talked with Jeff Johnson about the rest of the summer. Right now it looks like I'll be a "Gail".

(Ask John what she did). $350 for the whole summer. I'm living in Wilfong Lodge probably the whole summer.

Garden Grove is up now and it's mostly little girls. Hopefully by the end they'll get some good ones. Can't wait for Pasadena to come up so there will be someone I know up here. That's all that has happened so far. I'll have a lot of spare time so you'll probably get several letters.

(signed) Me

July 9, 1973

Moms and Pops:

Hi, thought I'd write because it's my day off. I've lived in tent-cabins all week. I'm the lake man now and I won't get more money unless I get my social security # so please send it up. Also, a note saying I can be operated on, blah, blah, blah, and sign it. These things are vital so don't hesitate, please.

I'm having a great time, got the run of the camp and part of the kitchen. Tell Pat, Bill, Jeff, if they want to come up to make it a Saturday because it's my day off. I've been hiking around a lot and have found some neat stuff. I'll know the place by the end. I have no way of getting home, so don't expect me.

The guy who has archery owns a boat at Big Bear and last night we went water skiing before dark (Fri). By the end of the summer, I'll be pretty good. I've been doing a lot of reading and no writing. You have my permission to send any or all of the following items:

1. Boot laces
2. Shoelaces
3. Clothes (my Bluff Lake staff shirt get from Bill)
4. Money
5. Girls
6. A Car.

That's all for now.

July 19, 1973

Hello--

I got a few minutes, so I'll put down some notes. Today has been the worst day I've had all summer. Several boats got stuck and I'm dining hall steward, so any problems automatically come direct to me. Now it's only lunch and I still have most of the day to go. I hope I make it.

Tomorrow, I get payed—I hope. In two weeks, I might get to go home for a day. If you're coming up tell me so I can tell you what to bring. You might want to call. I still need more clothes besides what you sent up. Also, my stereo, records, tapes, speakers, etc.

Not much is really happening around here, just the same old routine day after day, week after week. The kids this week are pretty bad compared to ones I've seen.

I got a girlfriend. She lives in West Covina and was up here 2 weeks ago. She'll be back up as a counselor later and her name is Marci.

That's all for now, I got to go to work.

Love, Jac

Here is a post card from brother Jim to Jac with a picture of Korean dancers:

Seoul, 14 August 1973

Happy Birthday, Jac!

Here's a happy little party for you—not that they're celebrating your birthday (because they didn't know when it was!), but they are celebrating. These are the well-known masked dancers of Korea. They do a dance which makes fun of various kinds of people in society such as the nobles, the monks, the king. It's a kind of ancient satire.

 I got your note a while back—thanks—and I hope that your summer is restful and a good change of pace. I heard that you're up in the mountains at camp. It must be good to be in the freshness and quiet of nature again! I've been stuck in the capitol of Seoul for a while, but it hasn't prevented me from seeking out peaceful parks and other "summer places." I hope you are well in body and spirit.   Jim

Thursday, June 24, 1974

Dear Grandpa and Grandma:

 Greetings from Camp! I've been here a week now and I love it. I guess you just have to love kids to have a good time.

 I'm sorry this thank you is so late, but we (the staff) had 1 ½ days to open camp for 190 people. There are about 25 (hard working) staff members. For the first few days you hardly get a break, there's always something that needs doing.

 I'll be working on the archery range for a good part of the summer. I'm the archery instructor. I teach around 30 kids a day for 2 or 3 days at the beginning of each week. The rest of the week I watch them while they shoot. Most of the time it is a relaxing job.

I can really make good use of the money you gave me. I can use it here at the camp and some I'll need in San Diego, next year at school. It will come in <u>very</u> handy. Thanks a lot!

That's about all from here, Thanks again,

Love, Jac

November 12, 1974

Hello Everyone!

Life has been treating me well these days. Hope much of the same for you guys. This letter won't be long because I've been studying for 2 ½ hours and I'm about 2/3 finished. (I'm really tired of writing!). My classes are alright, I got an A-, B+ on a chemistry exam. Out of about 500 people I scored about 25 people from the "top". (Everybody else blew it).

Anyway, I worked out a schedule for the next couple of years and <u>maybe</u> I'll be able to take a photo class next semester. (Definitely if the English classes are filled.). I may be taking

18 units next semester so I'll need an easy one like photo or my head will explode.

Our house was doing fine until the girl who lived there moved out (Ann) raising my rent to $100 (Along with the others) for this month. We were planning on getting a new roommate but everybody that came over either we didn't like, or they didn't like us... so the 4 of us decided to terminate the lease at the end of this month. Finals don't end till the 20th of Dec., so I'll be without a home for 20 days.

I won't have any problem finding a place (like Uncle Tom's, or maybe Ann's at the beach) for that time but this month I'm going to run out of money earlier than expected, especially with the cost of fixing the house before we leave (rug shampooer, etc.) coming up. I'll need money around the 20th-25th, Dad, so I won't be able to pick it up at Thanksgiving, the 28th, but I will be up for 3 or 4 days.

Next semester I'll get a room in the dorms. This should be really easy, but studying will be impossible, I hear.

The weather has been great. It's about 85 degrees now and <u>very clear.</u>

Love, Jac

Monday, Feb. 18, 1975

Howdy Folks!

Well, the big news this week concerns my Chemistry class (2nd semester Gen. Chem). I've been going along O.K. as far as labs go and the ever-present quizzes (I only blew about half of the quizzes so far) and last week we had our first test. Out of about 700 people, I finished in the top 15 with a strong "A". That's my first A in Chemistry ever! It seems to be getting easier as we go along.

My other classes are going well also. A "B" on Math and Biology tests last week. None of these three tests were easy but I think I have some really good profs. And they make it easier.

I'm narrowing my job possibilities down to a few places. I visited the local Y.M.C.A. but it turns out it's only an office. (I guess to raise funds for a new branch) so I'm going to the main branch tomorrow. There is a huge apartment/hotel across the bay that may have weekend jobs available and I'm calling pool services to help clean pools. I'll write at the end of this week to give you the details.

The last money I received was $140 about 3 weeks ago, of which $80 went to rent and the rest has disappeared to the ridiculous food prices (or just prices period). My rent isn't till the 10th **so** $80.00 then would be helpful but I need food money now that I'm broke. If you could send it before Friday, I could get it Fri. or Sat. and not have to live off my roommates. All three of our budgets are extremely limited so we're always on the watch for good prices and we eat together nearly every night to cut costs.

I'll have to look at my school schedule in order to see about making it up to Sierra Madre, but I'll tell you in my next letter.

The weather has been rainy lately but it might clear up and get warm soon. … I hope. That's all for now. You should get another letter next week.

Love, Jac

P.S. I'm asking people if they would cut my hair but so far, no takers…My job may depend on it but then again…See ya later. Jac

March 6, 1975

Hi Everybody!

  I wasn't able to write two days ago because of schoolwork and job hunting. I have a test each day in Biology (twice a week), each day in Chem lab (twice a week) and the rest of my time is spent looking for, applying for, and following up on jobs. So far, I've looked at school each day when I get out (at the job board) and in the paper a lot. I've applied for gardening, painting, YMCA work and yesterday at this place called Foodmaker. It's a huge part of some corporation (they own Jack-in-the-Box) and they wanted routine lab work done. I'm qualified but it'll depend on the hours they need filled.

  I wasn't able to get painting-gardening jobs from school because you need a phone, so last Monday I ordered one and it came today, Thurs. They cost $50 to install (1/2 is a deposit, which I get back later) and that's why I didn't get one sooner!! Now I should get a job from school within a week, but naturally I'll keep looking around (pretty soon the ads have got to be in my favor!) Regular part time work is hard to find because of my long long hours at school, not to mention out of school.

I really did get my hair cut, and you may be able to notice when I come up in two weeks (If I'm not working!)

That is all for now. My number is 714-224-8461.   Love, Jac

May 4, 1975

Howdy,

With school coming to an end soon, much is happening these days. It's to the point where I have to schedule time to sleep! Which, as it turns out, I'm doing a barely adequate job of. I just went through a week of testing and today I was finally able to take a day off: except that the weather report was correct and the sun hasn't been out for hours.   It's so cold outside everybody is running around with shoes on! (In May!)

Yesterday was Kregg's (not Mikes) birthday. A friend of his gave him a white, month-old dove. So far it has spent more time out of the cage than in.... I'm pretty sure he likes it. We made him (her!) several perches to sit on using string and pieces of wood and all the hooks we have on our ceiling. We just made him a new one and it took him about 30 seconds to learn how to swing on it.

For a while the bird didn't know how to fly too well, but today he made a perfect landing on the arm of one of our chairs. He used to stop (rather abruptly) by running into a wall.

Like I said, I took a couple tests last week. One in Chemistry and one in Math. The math test hasn't been returned yet, but the chemistry test (last one before finals) was easy. This whole semester in Chemistry has been much less hassle than first semester. Taking the tests have become easier because I know what to study. Instead of studying all of the stuff a little, it's better to study a little of the stuff a lot. This last test I did just that and got 29 out of 30. This may have clinched an "A". Bio and Math will be B's. There's no telling Mexican-American Studies and bowling.

I went through my second day on the job yesterday. Most of my "patients" are 65 to 85 with an occasional youngster or two around 62 or 60. I think the oldest was 88! Wow, are these people something. Anyway, it's fun and the pay is not bad. We start at 8:00 on Saturday morning and finish when all the people that are signed up get through all the tests. We do hearing (my job at the moment), sight, ECG, blood and urinalysis tests on everybody (for free if necessary).

Hearing tests are interesting to give to people (especially <u>these people</u>) but in a couple weeks I'll probably be doing something with a little more action. As it is, I'm stuck in this little room <u>all day.</u> The pay works out to about $2.60 an hour.

I'll be dropping by within 2 weeks.... See ya then,

Love, Jac

Saturday, August 2, 1975

Hi Everybody!

You wonder why I haven't written? Part of the reason is that it is summer and I don't write anything when it's summer. I have to re-learn every Fall. There are a few other reasons, but what can I say? I blew it.

Let me give you a quick rundown on what I've been doing for 2 months down here. On Monday, Tuesday, Thursday, and Friday, I get up at 5:30 in order to leave at 6:30. I get to work at 6:45. My boss and I arrive at our first place at 7:00. We do from 3 to 5 places before noon with one 5-minute break (besides travel time). We take an hour for lunch and work straight on until 5-5:30. That's 10-10 1/2 hours and I get paid (everyday) $18-$19, $2 an hour for 9 hours (because I don't get paid for lunch).

I drive home by 6:00 but usually don't eat until around 7:00 which leaves me all of 2 ½ hours until 9:30 when I hit the sack in order to get the necessary 8 hours sleep. Saturday, I work ½ day (and often recuperate by sleeping the other half. That leaves Sunday and Wednesday for shopping, clothes washing and beach going.

You all heard we have 2 cats now, didn't you? Well, recently a friend of ours came over with a new 4-wheeler he just bought so we all went across the street to see it only to find our cat's brother (who lives in the back with some other friends) running around on the other side.

Naturally, we picked him up to carry him back when all in our party except me ran back across (I hesitated too long). The next thing I knew our cat darts out right in front of a car going at least 25. The people threw on the brakes, but hit the cat with the front tire going in a skid. Sabu (his name) was thrown 20 feet ahead by the impact and (I guess) narrowly misses getting hit a 2nd time by the same car, which passed but later came back.

Sabu then was in a total state of confusion and winding up in the middle of the road made a go for the other side, only this time, again, another car was coming the other direction. I'm not sure if he made contact with it but he did go underneath it as it passed. This car didn't stop at all. When we finally brought him upstairs, he came out with no broken bones, no skin injuries, in fact the only mark on him was on his hip near his tail where he got hit the first time by the skidding tire, where the fur was ruffled and slightly discolored. Still, it took him quite a while to recover completely from the shock. **AMAZING, huh? Absolutely, unbelievable.** I had a hard time convincing everybody what had really happened.

One last note: I'll be up when I get off work in mid-August. Tony and I may be able to go up together. (We can split the cost, heh, heh!)

Love, Jac

September 3, 1975

Howdy!

Well, school is in full swing now. My schedule is working out pretty good, even though, as usual, I'm not taking many of the classes I registered for. Good system, eh?! Oh well, it usually works out in the end. On Monday, Tuesday, and Thursday I go until almost 5:00 starting at 9:00 a.m. on Monday and 8:00 a.m. the others. Wednesday and Friday I go at 9 and only have 2 classes. The second one goes from 12 to 1:00.

My classes are:

1. Chemistry (with 1 day Lab)

2. Chemistry Lab (another day; total 2 days lab)

3. Physics (a new class for Pre-med, etc.)

4. English (composition-reading-ugh!)

5. Geography (need something like this to graduate)

6. Physics Lab (separate class from lecture)

7. Archery (twice a week, for an hour)

Believe it or not, all this comes to only 16 units. I can see now how college is going to be a long haul. I could have taken some biology, but I have to take English, etc. sometime.........

I've got a 12:00 class in a while. The weather has been real real good (right when school begins) lately...sunny every day.

Love, Jac

Dec. 9, 1975

Hello Everybody!

Today begins the last week of this semester, except for finals. As you can guess, I'm very busy. I spent the entire weekend studying chemistry for my last test in there on Tuesday (tomorrow) before the final. My only final is in chemistry and the schedule says it will be on Thursday, the 18th. At least I'll have enough time to prepare for it. My other class's tests are all this week. Physics and Geography on Friday, Archery (if you can believe that!) on Thursday; my English class has papers due, but I don't consider that a final, and both

Physics and Geography have non-comprehensive last tests.

Today, like yesterday, I'm spending all my time with chemistry; the dumb test is at 9:30 A.M.! Much, much too early. You have to be completely ready the night before. Then after that test is over, I have to start in on my chem-lab final which happens the next day. I think after this week is over, I could sleep for a month if it weren't for finals.

I have been working every week lately and am planning on working the next 2 Saturdays also. Last Saturday was wild at the clinic. We had people from the Ukraine (sp?), Bohemia, along with the usual crowd from Mexico, Spain, and Italy and even June Taylor. She came dancing in to have her lung capacity measured and I cracked up, even though we both knew she wasn't <u>the June Taylor.</u>

Rent is due tomorrow leaving me with about $35. I need about $50 to make it 'till I come home. I should be home on the 21st, probably not sooner. See you then. My class starts in 5 min.

Love, Jac

February 7, 1976

Howdy!

School is in full swing, now, and I'm just beginning to set up a pattern for study. My classes are:
1. Organic chemistry (2nd semester)
2. Chem Lab (2nd semester)
3. Physics
4. Physics Lab
5. English (Last semester of this)
6. Human Physiology

Believe it or not, these are the ones I registered for and I'm actually going to take them. First-time I won't have to go through the rig-a-ma-roll of Add-Drop. None of the microbiology courses were open when I registered, so I decided on the physiology class. In it we'll be studying most of the general body systems and metabolic reactions. It's a straightforward lecture and won't cause too many problems.

The Physics class is the same one I took last semester (2 semester Physics with applied calculus), and got an "A" in. Similarly, my English teacher is the same one I had in the fall, who I think gave me a "B". The Chemistry class is the same one I took, only this time, my lecturer is also my lab instructor, in my section. What a break.! Any questions I need answered about lectures I can have cleared up during the 6 hours of lab a week. (Usually a good student runs the lab.) My schedule is quite a bit like last semester. **I expect** to do a little better this time, though. I haven't got my grades from last semester yet, but when I do, I'll send them up.

It has been raining down here for 5 days! This is the longest storm they've had since I've been here. That is, if you call 5 days of drizzle a storm. We get a 4-day weekend next week, for Lincoln and Washington's birthdays. I haven't made any plans yet, but I'm thinking of a trip to the desert or Mexico. It depends on who around here wants to go where.

The Saturday clinic is still operating, despite the doctor mess, etc. Today was quite hectic. We had all these observers and people-in-training today. At times, with all the patients and the others, it seemed like the walls were going to burst!

The morning didn't begin too smoothly either. Steve (a co-worker who lives in my building) and I drove out to work early to have breakfast at this place about 5 blocks from the clinic. I left my lights on during breakfast and of course, the car wouldn't start until after work when the battery had rested. We were only slightly late and wet when we arrived at the clinic.

Not much else has been happening around here. People are not unhappy about the rain. Perfect weather can become monotonous too. I've started sewing my mountain parka this week, but had so many problems putting in a zipper that I didn't touch the thing today.

Kregg has been thinking of moving to a different place (any place would be an improvement!) but hasn't found one yet. We'll let you know if we do find a place.

That's all! Love,
Jac

3-1-76

Hi Everybody!

I got the results back on my first Physics test the other day. I was #2 in the class with a 95% (#1 got 100%). So much for the good news...now for the bad news: Last Friday I was in the library when some sneaky s.o.b. stole my calculator! What a drag!! It was in my pack. When I left to look up something and a minute later when I came back it was long gone. O well, that's the breaks. I should make it ok. for a while without, but figuring on homework, etc. was so much easier when I had it. They're coming out with so many inexpensive new ones these days, that mine would have been useful for a few years, but I'm sure I can pick up another like it for 1/3 to 1/2 the cost we paid. Enough of the bad news.

I took a chemistry test last week and I should be getting those results back tomorrow. I think I got an 85% or so. That would be an "A". This semester I'm shooting for straight A's, and if I keep up, I should make it with no problem. If I do get all A's, it'll be the first time!

I got my admission notice from Santa Barbara the other day, which means they got my application, but nothing else. Now I have to wait a while until they go over my record. I'm really looking forward to a change of scenery, and especially a small school. This place gets to be a mad house very often. (not to mention a ripoff joint)

My money situation is holding o.k. but rent is due next week and $250 should last me through March. I'm running again, and trying to eat well, too. It's raining today, down here.

Love, Jac

Mon, Jan 19, 1975

Howdy. from Diego!

Just a short note to inform you of my present activities, etc. I made it down here OK, except for when my car stalled. Every time it gets hot, if I shut off the engine, it will not start again. If I get off the freeway after driving a while I don't dare shut off the engine, or I may be delayed a couple hours! I'm asking around to see what might be wrong with it.

I have one more week of vacation left, then it's back to the books. Deciding what classes to take hasn't been easy. If I get into Santa Barbara, I'd rather take the general education courses there, since I'm not going to want to take History, English, etc. here if it won't transfer. I'm playing it safe and taking those kinds of courses at the school I'm graduating from. I know I don't want to take those courses twice.

Therefore, I've decided to take only courses I want to take. So far, I've decided on Chemistry and Physics. I may take a Genetics course or a Microbiology course. (Depends on which is open). To finish off the units, I may take a health class (an elective).

I register on Thursday, this week. I'll write another letter then to tell you how I made out. Before I register, however, I need money. It's $95 just to get your classes. Feb. rent will be due soon after school starts and I will have a couple of books to buy. To last me through Feb. I figure I need at least $250 in the bank. I need this money by Friday, the 23rd at the latest. If you receive this on Wednesday, send a check right away and I should get it by Friday.

I'm still working at the clinic on Saturday, and I'm starting to recopy old, important chemistry notes so I'll be ready when school starts.

I may be coming up around the first, but I'll have to wait to see if its definite.

That's all for now!

Love, Jac

September 29, 1976

Hello!

Almost a week gone by...seems like three! Each day so many things happen it's hard to believe. The hall I live in is full of return customers. We've sponsored two parties already and another one is tonight. They're paying off though, since the girls in another hall have invited us (and I hope only us) to a picnic this weekend. Things ought to settle down next week when classes start.

Today I went down to the year-book office to sign up for a place on the Photographers staff. I'm almost positive I'll be on it which means I not only get access to the dark room, but film, paper, and chemicals are free!! I'll know more about it next Tuesday.

Refrigerator rental is $60 a year or $25 a quarter. Since you can take food out of the commons (cafeteria) and since the hours the commons are open are too short, this refrigerator deal is looking better and better.

My classes are still not confirmed except for genetics (with the book written by the co-discoverer of **DNA**, James Watson) and math with a **HUGE** book that costs about $20. I might get a class called Neurobiology (all about the nervous system) or Microbiology.

There are lots of chicks around this place, lots of good-looking ones...oooowheee!

(Ginny's note: Jac met his first wife Belinda the first week he was in Santa Barbara. I told him it was because of the good haircut I gave him.)

Do you remember the banana social? Well, it was a huge success. Everybody came just to see what could possibly happen at something called a "banana social".

The first day I lived in the dorms several people stopped by the room to see how Bob and I got one of the best rooms in the whole place! We told them we didn't know and I think they went away a little disillusioned about the priorities for room assignments. Oh, well, we're just lucky, I guess. So far, the location has and hasn't paid off. The parties are right next door along with the showers, but the clouds haven't broken up all week so the view has been limited. Someday we'll see the coastline to the south and maybe the mountains and the Channel Islands also. Who knows?

After buying books and supplies my monetary resources will be seriously depleted. I'd like to open a bank account so I can cash checks. I'm not sure how much I'll need but anywhere from $50 to $100 should last fairly long and then I'll be able to better gauge my expenses next quarter.

Chrissy Brown **(our neighbor in Sierra Madre)** just called and she said that she got my neurobiology class. Also, I just missed lunch while

I was here doing my wash, now you see why I need that refrigerator? That's all,

Love, Jac

My address: P.O. Box 12129

UCSB, Santa Barbara, CA 93106

Phone: 968-7739 (805)

October 27, 1976

Hello!

Lots happening around here <u>all the time</u>! Last night I developed 8 rolls of film. First time I've used the darkroom here (since the head of the yearbook couldn't get keys to us). If you've never developed 8 rolls of film at once... Don't!! The darkness (total), chemicals (stinky), and developing tanks (difficult to use, even when you can see, which you can't) all add together and spell: bummer. Combined with the fact that I got a badly sprained foot (I can limp) made the four-hour test of developing endurance barely tolerable.

The sprained foot came in an intramural football game (which we lost 12 to 0). That's the last game I'm playing in. We have nobody who can pass, catch, or run. Too bad.

I went rock-climbing last Saturday up in the local hills here. I met this guy with a really nice rope, and the minimal amount of equipment to top rope. (Tony can explain.)

We brought (actually she drove us) this girl I met and she made a nice climb (about 15 feet) and learned how to rappel (sp?) and loved it! Boy, was I surprised! I made a nice 100 ft. climb up an 80 degree to 85-degree rock face. I also rappelled down, just to freshen up on this technique. Jeff also made the climb I did.

My first test I got a B on. That was calculus, which I despise, so can't expect much better. Try to do better next time...Took another test in Genetics and think I did pretty good. Haven't gotten that one back yet. My other class Neurobiology) doesn't have a test until next week. My entire quarter consists of only 7 tests (finals included) so if you blow it on one or two.......

My roommate is really cool. He brought up a huge stereo with 4 huge speakers. Then he brought up a guitar (he's from Redlands and goes back about every other week!) His taste in music is radically different than mine, so we have a lot of variety.

The weather has been up and down, but yesterday and today are beautiful. I'm gonna catch some rays for sure today. My schedule (class time) is fairly light with only 3 classes. 4 days of the week, I have only 2 classes to go to. Monday I have 3, that's why I'm getting involved in all these extra activities, even though I can tell they're affecting my studying time.

My classes are <u>difficult</u>. I can barely understand my Neurobiology class. (which in case you didn't know, is about the entire nervous system from the subcellular to cellular to the organismal level) so far all we've studied has been cell membranes! My Genetics class is 90% chemistry (all about **DNA**) so my background in that has helped me. Calculus is...well, calculus.

From what I've seen of dorm people and life, I'd say, "good thing I don't have to live here to go to school here.

More on this later...

Love, Jac

P.S. Thanks for the cash and pictures. I like those pictures too!

21 Jan. 1977

Howdy!

Things have been going really good these days. My classes are all at good times. Monday, Wednesday, and Friday I go until 12 (only two classes) and I have one class in the morning and lab in the afternoon the other two days. My classes are Philosophy 1, Neuro-biology lecture and lab and math.

Philosophy is pretty interesting. It's like a self-instruction class, the lectures don't have anything to do with the grades, since there are no tests, only papers about a subject you decide on, research, etc. The Prof. doesn't help you with your subject (The T.A.s do) he just talks about the philosophical problem he's working on. The lectures are optional (since there is no real subject matter in the course) but I've been to them all since the guy is interesting to listen to and it costs a fortune to go to school up here.

My math class is really difficult. I'm already lost completely on Chapter 1. This is the last course I'll take in math. It's the first upper division math course I've taken and its hard core. I'll get a "B" if I work on it a lot.

My Neurobiology class is really great. We're learning neural mechanisms (which nerve fires when and why) for intact animals when they respond to a stimulus. For example, why does a cockroach scurry under something when lights are turned on, which nerves are firing, and what internal effect does this have: which muscles contract, which relax, in order for the cockroach to make it to safety. We work with crabs, flies, these large slug-like things called sea-hare, and cockroaches in lab.

This is my first work at dissection and I'm terrible. Luckily my lab-partner is a graduate student and has done a lot of this kind of work He's a lousy experimentalist and doesn't know anything about electronics so we make a great team: with my electronic knowhow and my imagination for thinking up tests to run, and him doing all the delicate surgery our experiments are working out really well. Last Thursday I spent 5 hours in the lab working on sea-hare brains. They look like this:

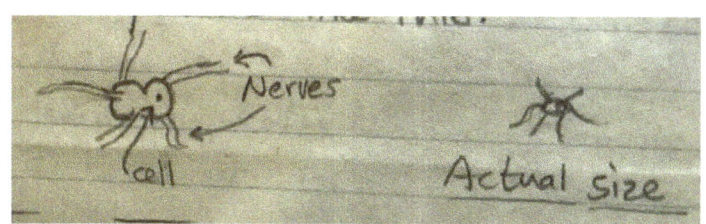

(picture of sea-hare brains)

Tony: Call up Linda and Lori and tell them I need their addresses. We get a 3-day weekend in a little while and I'd like to have them come up for a visit. Send quick!!!!!

Also, Tony, there are no rocks to climb here at all. Probably the closest place is Stoney Point. We might want to work out a day to meet there, but I'll need directions, so send them up, and I'll work on it. Also, Pinnacles National Monument is happening. It's about 3 hours from here, so think about cruising up sometime and we'll take off from here. I haven't had time to do any J.T. pictures, but someday I'll have proof sheets so you can see what you want to have enlarged.

My grades last quarter were:
Neurobiology. . . . A-
Calculus . . . . A-
Genetics . . . . A-
Total G.P.A.   3.70

That's the highest G.P.A. I've ever had. If I can get through my present math class, this quarter's G.P.A. should be about the same. Note: we don't' get 4.0 for an A-, just 3.7. You have to get an A to get 4.0 (But A+=4.3 so if I get a couple of those, It'll even out some of the A-'s).

I'm completely broke from buying books and photocopying material in the library, plus other living expenses. When I move out, I'll need quite a bit of money for rent, deposit, etc. but for now I only need a about $50 to make it through the quarter. The dorms are as noisy as ever... Bob and I are going nuts around here....

Love, Jac

P.S. Somebody took my new Christmas pants. Mom, if they turn up, hide 'em! I'll bring John's back in a few weeks. Jac

After graduation from the University of California at Santa Barbara, Jac married Belinda in our backyard. They moved to Boulder, Colorado, where Jac studied and received his PhD in microbiology. Their son Brad was born in 1982 and Lauren was born in 1983.

Starting In 1984 Jac worked for 2.5 years at Scripps Clinic and Research foundation In La Jolla, California, his first postdoc position. Then he moved to Los Alamos (affectionately known as Lost Almost by the locals) for another 2.5 years for his second postdoc.

Jac moved to Boston for his first faculty position at Harvard School of Public Health (Dept. of Cancer Biology in 1990. He divorced Belinda and married Debra. We received the following letter from Jac with the letterhead:

**HARVARD UNIVERSITY
SCHOOL OF PUBLIC HEALTH
LABORATORY OF RADIOBIOLOGY
BOSTON, MASSACHUSETTS**

June 5, 1990

Hi!

Thought you might like to see the new house, now that we've moved in. I bought a lawn mower last weekend--Just in time, since the grass was over a foot tall. I also got my first paycheck and made my first mortgage payment, so I guess it really is "our house."

Work couldn't be better. I've managed to convince the powers that be that I needed 750 sq. ft. rather than the standard 500, and my graduate student (Wing Ping Deng) from Taiwan, he goes by the name "Weber") and my technician, Doug, have begun some experiments.

I can't thank you guys enough for all you've done for me. The move to Boston couldn't have gone any smoother, and the new house is wonderful to come home to after work.

So far Boston is a fun place to be. Deb and I have gone to Indian, Thai, & Chinese restaurants. All have been very good. She comes back to Boston in about two weeks for about 2 weeks. Then she starts her last year.

The kids arrive with Lola (my Mom) *on August 2. They sound pretty excited about seeing the new home.*

Love, Jac

Jac's family left Boston for the University of New Mexico Medical School in 1996. He became chair of Molecular Genetics and Microbiology Department (17 faculty) in 1998 and stayed in that position until 2006. Jac moved to Fort Collins, Colorado, as chair of Environmental and Radiological Health Sciences (40 faculty) in 2008 and stayed in that position until 2019. He is still a professor in that department.

Jac has edited three volumes *of DNA Damage and Repair* in 1999: *Volume 1: DNA Repair in Prokaryotes and Lower Eukaryotes; Volume II: DNA Repair in Higher Eukaryotes; Volume III: Advances from Phage to Humans.* He edited *Breast Cancer Molecular Genetics, Pathogenesis and Therapeutics;*

Chemokines and Cancer. No way could I understand any of these volumes.

Jac and Belinda's son Brad lives in California. He and Melissa have two sons, Maxtone (10) and baby Teddy. Brad homeschools Max.

Their daughter, Lauren, is married to Scott McFall. They have a daughter, Clementine (3).

Lauren is a marketing project manager and podcast producer. Her husband Scott is an audio engineer. They both work in their home. Clementine is their daughter (3). They live in Ashville, South Carolina.

Jac and Debra's daughter Brielle was born in 1995 in Boston. Daughter Alexa was born in 1999 in Albuquerque.

Debra graduated from medical school while they lived in Boston. She had a residency in pathology at Harvard and later became faculty at Harvard. In Colorado she is on the faculty in the dept of Microbiology, Immunology in the College of Veterinary Medicine and Biological Sciences at the same school as Jac. Her main role is co-director of the CSU Infectious Disease Research Center.

Both daughters Alexa and Brielle have very good jobs. Brielle was a founder of a small start-up company based on voice technology and she and her colleagues sold their company to a large Fortune 500 company, which hired her as part of the sale and where she continues to work. She just launched an AI-based voice product for that company. She lives in San Francisco.

Alexa works for a large website design company, in the technical writing and education areas. She writes the instructions for new tools that the company develops, and she also helps with the video productions of the education group in that company. Alexa lives in Fort Collins, Colorado.

On June 28, 2023, a happy Grandma Ginny received the following greeting card from granddaughter Brielle accompanying a beautiful painting she made for me. I'm pairing it on the wall with another abstract painting she made for me. Here is the accompanying note:

Hi Grandma!

I miss you! I created this painting and thought I'd send it over to you. It reminds me of the ocean!

I hope you're having fun and enjoying summer. It's never summer here in San Francisco

I love you! Brielle

Chapter Eight

No. 5 son Tony (Antoni Dmitri) typed a beautiful letter to my mother when her husband Les passed away: 12/10/88.

GRANDPA LES WAS A VERY KNOWLEDGEABLE AND AWARE MAN.

HE WOULD ALWAYS BE READING OR WATCHING THE NEWS, AND HE REALLY LIKED HIS MUSIC …HE ONCE GAVE ME A GUITAR IN BRAND NEW CONDITION THAT WAS OLDER THAN I WAS WHEN I WAS 25.

AS A KID, I REMEMBER GRAMPA WORKING IN THE GARAGE ALWAYS BUILDING OR FIXING SOMETHING. HE COULD FIX ANYTHING!!! I REMEMBER CONSTRUCTING THE HUGE BLOCK WALL OUT BACK BY THE ALLEY WHERE ALL THE LITTLE BLACK KIDS WERE ALWAYS PLAYING. THEY ALL LOVED HIM VERY MUCH TOO.

WHEN IT CAME TO CARS, HE WAS AN EXPERT…FROM. WORKING ON LOCOMOTIVES. HIS AND (LOLA'S) MOTORHOME WAS A TECHNICAL WONDER FOR ITS TIME. HE HAD ALL THE SPECIAL

GAUGES IN FRONT OF HIM AND YOU BOTH WORE NAVY BLUE SHIRTS WITH PILOT AND CO-PILOT TAGS ON THE FRONT.

GRANDPA AND I HAD LOTS OF INTERESTING TIMES IN RECENT YEARS PRODUCING MANY ELABORATE TELEVISION "SHOWS" OF LOLA PLAYIING THE DRUMS.... COMPLETE WTH STEREO SOUND, LIGHTING, MICROPHONES, TRIPODS, CABLES RUNNING EVERYWHERE, AND HE WAS THE TECHNICAL ENGINEER, THE CAMERAMAN, THE SOUNDMAN. ALL I WAS WAS HIS GRIP. SOME TAPES INCLUDE CLOSE-UPS OF LOLA PLAYING AS MANY AS 3 AND 4 DIFFERENT INSTRUMENTS AT THE SAME TIME

HE WAS AN AVID SPORTS FAN OF ALL MY BROTHERS AND MYSELF.

HE WOULD OFTEN COME WATCH ME PLAY FOOTBALL, ALWAYS WITH CAMERA INHAND...I DON'T THINK I REMEMBER HIM NOT HAVING A CMERA ALONG WHEREVER HE WAS.

WHEN LOLA AND LES MOVED TO APPLE VALLEY, HE FINALLY GOT HIS "RANCH" COMPLETE WITH A FRUIT ORCHARD. BETWEEN LES, LOLA, JON, DAD, AND ME WE FINALLY GOT THE WATER

SYSEM TO WATER EACH AND EVERY TREE, INCLUDING A FEW TREES WE PLANTED.

GRANDPA WAS ALSO A FRIEND. SOMEBODY WHO BELIEVED IN ME AND MY TELEVISION STRUGGLES. HE THOUGHT I HAD A GREAT NAME FOR A DIRECTOR.

I APPRECIETE ALL THAT HE DID FOR ME IN HOLLYWOOD, VISITNG ME AT THE STUDIO SOMETIMES WHILE BUYING GRANDMA SOMETHING FOR HER DRUMSET…

IT SEEMS LIKE YESTERDAY

I LOVED HIM AND AM GREATFUL FOR THE TEACHER IN HIM BECAUSE HIS INFLUENCE WILL BE WITH ME THE REST OF MY LIFE,

YOUR GRANDSON,

Tony

I have a Mother's Day card that Tony made for me in his early grades of school. It is manila size and he pasted paper flowers on it and one flower blossom says: "Happy Mother's Day."

My Mom

She is a good Mom. When she is nice, and when I want to play dice, and when she sees some mice, she goes and cries. She is nice when I want her to make rice. I love Mom.

Love, Tony, Sierra Mesa Room 8

Tony wrote this letter to his brother Jim dated March 11, 1969. He was 10 years old.

Dear Jim,

I am going to San Pedro on March 27, 1969, from 9 am to 2 pm. It is science you know. I am going with my class at school. We have only one race car and two motorcycles now. (My husband had a law case involving three teenage boys who stole a bag of money from a farmer in Georgia. The boys bought three Shelby racing cars, three motorcycles and three typewriters. Jimmy had to keep the 'evidence' while the lawsuit was pending. One day Jac (about 9 years old) came running in the front door and a policeman came right after him and asked me if I knew that little kid was riding a big Harley motorcycle. He would like to speak to him. Jac had locked himself in the bathroom.)

Tony's letter continues:

It is spring now. It snowed yesterday on the mountain, but we did not go up. I have glasses now, that's why I could not see the chalkboard. I hear you are coming home in 21 days from now. I got my picture taken 5 days ago. I'm writing this at school. Do you have my posters yet?

Mom is coming in 2 days. She is getting Jac some sandals and me some cards from every country.

Jonie Bear (our cat) is fatter than anything and Pepper Bear is skine. Pat's cat just had more babies. They have 1 black cat, 2 gray cats just like Jonie Bear and one black and white one. I am in a 4th-5th class, you know, I am in Mr. Singer's class. He is a good teacher, and I like him. I am doing a project on bones and musels. Bye now, be sure and write.   Love, Tony

A letter from brother Jim:

Andong, Sept. 9, 1971

Dear Tony,

I'm sorry this is going to get to you a little late (at least I think it will) but it's the thought that counts anyway. Happy #12! Are you really twelve years old? It's hard to believe!

I received your letter when I got back to Andong. Thanks. I always enjoy your letters---and except for Mom, you write me the most.

I've been in Andong a week now and I'm beginning to get back in the groove—which means it's not as fun as the vacation was. It's nice to see the students again, but the confusion at the school is so bad!

I'm sending you a couple pictures of the market in Andong. As you can see, I don't mean a super-market. This market is located outside on the street, not in a building. It's not the cleanest market in the world, but as long as you wash the things when you get home, I guess it's o.k.

One of the pictures shows a fish market; it's right behind that first fish stand that I play the piano every week. I guess the fish business is good because the people can afford a piano and also a television and a telephone!

In the other picture you can see the theater in the background. It's advertising a Chinese movie. Chinese movies are always the same: lots of blood and guts—I know you'd like them a lot.

Well, Happy Birthday again! Your brother Jim

Tony's Christmas Thank You letter to his Grandma Lola and Les:

February 7, 1976

Sierra Madre, Ca.

Dear Grama, and Grampa,

Thanks for all the clothes you gave me for Christmas. I sure used them this winter. Sorry for the long delay in getting this letter off to you but I've been kind of busy with changing schools and all that I didn't think about it.

Thanks again for everything and maybe I'll see you soon.

Your grandson, Tony

3-10-78   Basalt, Colorado

Hello from the North Slope of the Elk Range. I've had three excellent days of downhill skiing, cross-country skiing (broke the tip off my ski) and yesterday I hiked to the top of Basalt Mountain only to find a herd of 60 or more deer and an outrageous vista point.

I had gotten some maps (topographic) so we picked out all the 14,000 ft peaks we could see (11 of them in all) and took many pictures. On Wed. I cross-country skied from Aspen Village to Snowmass Village, only about 10 miles, but right before the summit, I fell in some <u>deep</u> powder. At first, I couldn't figure out how I was going to get out! Finally, when I did get out my left ski was a foot shorter. So slowly but surely, I traversed my way down many suicidal slopes wondering about tomorrow--no, not really but after I got down, I found out that they have temporary ski tip extensions that you can buy for $2.50--Time to read more books.

    Anyway, the reason I've had these three days off is because I quit my job at the Crestwood Lodge. But today I started working at the Holiday Inn by the Aspen Airport with plans to take on another job in downtown Aspen. A few things you need to know, or I need to know are listed on back:

    1. The Aspen-Basalt K.O.A. Emergency number: 927-3532 area code 303

(After 4:00 pm)

    2. When are you coming up and how? Also are you going up to see Tom, too?

3. Does Jac want to come up? Tell him to write.

4. Tell Tom to contact me -- (about a job!).

That's about it for now--anyway you should come up before April 9 because that's when the season ends. So long for now to the people I know on the western slope of the Sierra Nevada.

Tony

To any Nickoloffs at home & Grandpa Tanny,

March 13, 1978

Hello, Everybody,. . .

Just thought I'd tell you what I'm doing with my time (besides fishing, hiking, climbing.)

I just started working on the Phillips Ranch, which includes: Burning, digging irrigation ditches, fixing fences, digging wells, driving the tractor (not easy) and other assorted chores.

Anyway, the big news is that Con Phillips has a four-wheel drive truck for sale. Here's some info on it: 1. Good tires

2. 1 1/4-ton cherry 350 engine

3. Only 45,000 easy driven miles (it was. owned by an old guy who died and it was given to Con.

4. Heavy duty bumpers front and back

5. Spotlight on the roof.

Well, I'm on lunch right now and gotta get going, so I hope everybody is feeling well, and I'll see you all in June.

Tony

P.S. Tell Jimmy B. to get ahold of me or send me his number. Also, I forgot to tell you Con's going to let me work the truck off...he wants $2700 for it. Bye everybody!

In 1978 Tony took a job in Aspen, Colorado. A letter from Tony:

Sept. 11, 1978

How's it seems like summer is already over, Fall got passed up, and winter is already here. 36 degrees last night, woke up to snow covered peaks this morning--time to have them turn the heat on once again and break out the winter clothes--sweaters, down parkas and long <u>underwear!</u>

I bought a pair of skis the other day. $10 is all they cost. They call them rock skis because they're used for early in the season skiing when the snow doesn't quite cover the whole mountain, you ski on rocks a lot of the time. The skis are beat, but I couldn't pass up the price.

Most of the pictures I sent were taken by Steve, except the one of me standing in front of the ski slopes which was taken by this religious friend of mine--a real nice guy, maybe you will meet him someday.

Some other magazines also included for you to read and a few pamphlets on Grass Roots. The Aspen magazine tells about the Design Conference which is the program I worked with Grass Roots on. I had lots of fun (main thing) and also worked with good people and learned an awful lot, all at the same time.

Well, that's about all the news for now, I hope Mom and Jac come up soon and maybe even get the whole crew up here this winter. You all would love it! Just think, a white Christmas. Plus you can breathe some clean air for a while....

Tony

Jac did go to Aspen, and he got a job working at a hotel. Besides the above jobs, Tony videoed people on the slopes. They lived in a trailer they called the yellow submarine because it had a round window on the door. Both boys got mononucleosis. Jac went to Boulder where his girlfriend Belinda was working. Tony called me because he was sick and hungry, and nobody would come near him. I asked my doctor if I would get mono and he said that I was healthy and wouldn't. So, I flew to Denver and changed planes for Aspen. I asked the stewardess how many planes Rocky Mountain Airways had, and she said, "We had two until last week when it crashed." Now it is referred to as Rocky Mountain Scareways.

October 16, 1978

Hello,

*Well, here it is, the long awaited Thank you card--*THANK YOU!! *And Mom, thank you for coming up and Dad thank you for being my Dad. O.K. now that all the mushy stuffs over with, let's get down to business.*

Jac and I have been doing a little climbing and a little backpacking and I do mean a little. Three days off in the last month. Anyway, we've

(I) have saved some of that money and we're going to buy an old potbelly stove, only $50 bucks, actually brand new! About another 20 or 30 dollars to install it, but we will do that ourselves.

Jac did some remodeling to the place when I was at work. Looks Great!!! We've got a couch-bed combo and the stereo up high against the wall. Lots of room and when we get the wood burning stove in, this place is going to be deluxe.

Hopefully it will snow soon, so we can do some skiing, both downhill and cross-country skis are ready and so am I, and so is Jac, and so is everybody up here!

As it looks now, things should start coming together for winter jobs for both Jac and me, and maybe even a little vacation in between jobs for me. During this time, I'm going to look into another trailer that I could sub-rent so it will pay for itself!

Well, that's about it for now, so once again Thanx and I'll talk to you before you come up for Christmas. Your enterprising son, Tony

October 31, 1978

Howdy Everybody!

Just a short note to tell you thanx for all the money. We've been busy as bees around here, fixing this and that, narrowing down all the home improvements. Sorry to say there is some good news and some bad news. First the good news. With the extra money we've finished off the stove, complete with stone floor, brick walls and sheetrock backing (a fireproof substance). We also bought a deluxe chimney setup, with triple wall construction and many other added safety measures.

Also, with that money I've payed the doctor bill, and got a phone ordered.

With the rest of our spare time, we've collected more than a "cord" of wood—4X4X8) worth about $65 to $85 (free heat) is the way we look at it.

Here's the bad news--there's none! Right now we're still waiting on the people to move out. I think, by the time we've got this place (yellow submarine) 'cherryed out' it will be time to start on the new one.

By the way, this paper I'm writing on was left in the yellow sub when I moved in. Well, that's about it for me, Jac wants to say a few words, so, thanks again and I hope to hear from you soon...Tony

Hello, Tony has said just about everything--the present owner of the trailer is fixen the place up before he moves out so when we move in, it will be in great condition. More letters later,

Love, Jac

January 16, 1980

Howdy,

Thanks for sending the money, it almost pulled me out of the hole. If it wasn't for almost going off a cliff in the truck ($50 to get it towed) and my dog getting taken by the pound (Don't know how much that's going to cost... $25 for first offence plus number of days he's in. Still haven't gotten him out and it's been 3 days!)

I wanted to get a picture of the truck but didn't have any film or my video equipment with me.

Speaking of video... (and the good news) it's starting to work out pretty good. I shot the "Ski Splash" (Jumping into a swimming pool) yesterday and the town basketball league last night—total take for the whole day $60. Not too bad for a couple easy hours work.

The Basketball turned out well, except nobody came down. Uninteresting games I guess, so I'll probably wait until the playoffs in April.

I'm also going to do the hockey games coming up late this month. So far now, I got the free ski thing at the Timberline, the basketball games, the hockey games and <u>Private Tapes</u>, which is where the money is!

I'm at work right now, the dishwasher didn't show up. I'm going to cover for him tonight (cash).

As for the truck, it's running fine, and I finally got the new headlite in from when I hit that deer, plus I put the snow tires on.

I guess things are going well, although it could be flourishing if I could get those private tape sales going and didn't have to rely on odd jobs to get by. If I could direct all my energies toward the video, the kid's hockey games is a good one too, because (rich) parents could buy a tape of the game. Just like when you did my football games on super 8. Maybe sell one tape to two or three different parents, then I would rake in. Winter Skol is upon us, and I should be busy with all the activities going on. Bye for now...

Your son,
Tony

P.S. Oh yes, I went skiing last week. It was outrageous. 2 new feet of **POWDER**!

Brother Jim sent a letter to Tony from Korea dated:

Andong, September 7, 1972

Hey Tony!

I just finished a delicious lunch of dried fish, marinated fish, pickled cabbage, roots, and of course, rice—a standard lunch here at school. I usually take my lunch in a square box and the teachers all eat together, sharing each other's "goodies." Actually, it's not as bad as it sounds—**and what can** I say? After almost two years, it's become "normal" for me.

So, how are you on your……let's see….13th birthday? ("And the last little piggie reaches teenager-hood!"). I haven't heard much from you since my telephone calls home last July. Of course, I haven't heard much from anyone at home because I was a little "busy" and also I was in Japan for a couple weeks, but I imagine that by now you're getting excited (ha!) about school starting again. (An unfortunate coincidence---your birthday and the opening of school!)

For my part, I'm finally getting back into my normal routine, which isn't very much of a routine because things always seem to be so disorganized here. But school started a week ago—in Korea the kids get one month for summer vacation (August) and one month for winter vacation (January,) and I really think that if it weren't for the weather during these two months, they would have school twelve months a year!

I'm convinced you would hate the school system here, so be happy with what you've got! (Words of advice I know aren't necessary, but each time I walk into a classroom here—more like a prison than an educational institution—I think about the different atmosphere in an American school.)

(Right this minute I'm sitting in our school's library and about 8 kids are all crowded around me—staring and not believing that anyone could write like this. They really get a kick out of watching anyone write in English! Little do they know, of course, that the person I'm writing this to—namely you!—probably won't be able to read it anyway—just joking.)

As I look out the window, I can see the green hills on the other side of the river, the river, and then the green-green rice fields—and I am reminded that in another 3 weeks or so it will all begin to turn into gold! The gold of the rice harvest, and the red and orange of trees everywhere. Autumn is real in Korea and at this point I almost think the long cold winter is worth it for the spring, summer, and fall we have—but ask me again in December—and I'll probably be singing a different tune.

Oh, I have a question: did you ever get my letter about the pen-pal plan for your school and the school for deaf kids here in Andong? If so, do you think it would be possible to do it starting this fall? I hope so. If you don't know what I'm talking about, let me know and I'll explain it all again. The address, in case you lost it, is on the back of this page.

So that's it for now. I hope your birthday is great—and good luck in your fall projects!

Happy B-Day! Jim
Address: Korea 660
Kyung-buk, Andong City
Nong-A School (Pyoung Hwa Dong)

Brother Jim sent a letter to Tony from Jamaica on February 1, 1981:

Dear Tony,

It is a relatively cool, rainy day here today--the temperature is probably <u>down</u> to the upper 70's. There have been only 2 nights so far when it got below 70 degrees and that was 69. It's amazing to me how hot it is here, even in January.

This is just a note to say hello and to wish you well on the new business venture. Mom has kept me posted on things pretty regularly, so I know the difficulties you've had getting started. I'm sure it must be a little discouraging too at times. But don't give it up!

I'm slowly getting adjusted to life in Jamaica, though it will take a long time before I feel at home here. Working in this school is a bit of a trial for me--it's so disorganized and I feel like there's so much wasted time. But I'm beginning to make some friends outside of school, and I think many of the students like me, except for my one English class who act like I'm torturing them! But I'll press on...

Never done this before, but I'm writing to all four of you brothers today. Just want to stay in touch. Peace, Jim

While in high school, Tony took a class in video production at Pasadena City College and after graduation from high school, he worked in Hollywood for Music Contacts Service. He made videos of bands that they could use instead of live auditions. He also directed 50 episodes of "The Treehouse Kids," a live acting class on cable TV in Los Angeles. One of the students was Marlon Brando's daughter. He also directed seventy-five episodes of "L.A. Connection," a comedy improv, sometimes filmed on Venice Beach.

On one of his jobs, he was paid with two Actrix computers. I bought one of them. It was 1986 and brought me into the world of technology.

Working late one night in Hollywood, a gunman broke into the studio and held Tony up at gunpoint. This encouraged him to leave Hollywood and go to Atlanta where his brother Tom was expanding his restaurants.

In Atlanta, Tony had his own shows on People's TV and had a video repair business. He produced about 500 30-minute shows for an Indian which ran on Univision, a Spanish network. When the series ended, he worked for CBS News in Chattanooga.

Unhappy with the ruthlessness of the news business, Tony started working for brother Tom, becoming the company-wide media manager, setting up the menus, brochures, table tents and posters on the computer and creating the La Paz website. Creating websites became another occupation for Tony.

Tony married Jessie (Lai Kuen Leung) January 28, 2002. She had come to Atlanta from Hong Kong with a girlfriend. She trained to be a caregiver and in 2008, she and Tony moved in with me. Since I never enjoyed cooking, I was a happy camper and loved having a man in the house again since my husband had passed away in 1999, not to mention, finally having a daughter I never had!

It was wonderful having Tony to help me with the computer when I started writing books. He taught me how to do photoshop when I wrote the Granny with the Freckled Knees books and photoshopped my grandkids into my travels in Africa, Thailand and Egypt. He published these books for me on Amazon.

Sadly, we lost Tony with lung cancer in 2018. He was 59 years old. I am blessed to have his wife Jessie to take care of me. She works five days a week, but she always has my meals prepared and we love to go to restaurants on her days off and we play a lot of Mah Jong and scrabble together.

My three living sons, Jim, Tom and Jac started a five-o'clock wine time. They take turns calling me at 5 o'clock, at which time I'm supposed to have my glass of wine ready. This is kind of in honor of the many times my husband and I sat on our deck at five o'clock with a glass of wine, watching the "flotilla" of ducks swim by in the lake.

Jim lives in Miami, Jac in Colorado and Tom lives in north Georgia. When the boys are here, we sit on the deck at five o'clock with glass in hand.

Chapter Nine

My Mom also saved letters and copied some that I wrote to her that she put in her book:

A Grandmother's Life and

Her Family's

History and Genealogy

published in 1977.

Mom and Les were traveling all over the East and Mid-west in their motorhome gathering her genealogy information. That is why I was writing to her instead of phoning.

July 14, 1970 5 p.m.

Dear Mom and Les,

I have been writing bills since 3 o'clock so my writing hand is giving out, but thought this would probably be the last chance before you leave.

Haven't heard from Jim since he left Helsinki. John left for Mexico Saturday noon with Jack Simons. They will be gone for three weeks, then back for four days of good eating and then to Canada for three weeks.

Two days before John left, he received a letter from Long Beach State College saying he got the Resident Assistant job which pays $120 a month-- which covers his board and room and $20 a month extra for books. It was a load off our minds.

John has worked for me in the yard for 75 hours the last couple of weeks at $1.00 an hour, plus the $62.50 playing piano at the San Gabriel Civic Auditorium and $30 for playing at a Toluca Lake mansion at a fund-raising cocktail party for Ronald Reagan. He played three hours and played "California, Here I Come" for Reagan when he arrived. Jon shook hands with "Ronnie and Nancy" and Yorty, Mayor of Los Angeles.

He and Jack took enough groceries for 24 days plus tents, cots, formaldehyde to kill the lizards and bugs for his collection and a five-gallon water bottle, plus camera equipment and fishing poles and butter-fly nets. I don't know how the car moved under all that stuff! Haven't heard from him yet.

Sunday was a great day for the Nickoloffs-- at the award picnic Tony and Jac both got trophies and Tom won a 14-inch trophy for the highest batting average in the Colt League, a .409. The nearest to him was a .375.

When Tony's coach introduced him, he said, "If there is one family who dominated the trophies this year it is the Nickoloffs." Then after I played in the mother's game (short stop) and we lost 39-7 in three innings (called because of exhaustion), my husband and all the neighbors said I disgraced the name!

Tony's coach said that during one game Tony said to him, "Don't give me no signals coach 'cause I'm going to hit away!' So, the coach said, "When we straightened out who was the manager and who was the player—Tony went on to a good season hitting away".

Have a nice trip home.

Love, Ginny and family

Mom and Les are still traveling a year later.

August 25, 1971

Dear Mom and Les:

Today I am 39 for the 9th time and of all things to do on my birthday, we went to a funeral. Nick Vangel's wife Frosa. She was only 66 but she always looked 70 since I first met her 25 years ago--a real old country peasant woman with laughing sparkling eyes. After the burial at Forest

Lawn everyone went to the Barbecue (my father-in-law's restaurant) for lunch in the banquet room-- about 100 people including the priest. The whole service was in Bulgarian with lots of incense burning.

Jimmy is leaving tomorrow morning for Hawaii at 10 so I'll be coming in again (to L.A.) tomorrow morning to take him to the airport. He wanted to be there at least an hour early--says he doesn't want to miss this vacation with his sister Nada. I promised him I'd get in touch with Sheriff Pitchess and have a helicopter standing by in case we have car trouble.

Guess that paragraph was long enough. Jimmy B. always criticizes me for my paragraphing. I told him that's the way I think-- without paragraphs.

Haven't heard from you in a long time--did you get my letter at Sioux Falls? I can't tell where to send this until I hear where you are now.

We have had a very busy few days. Friday night we took Jac and Grandpa Nickoloff to Chasens Restaurant, a very fancy one in Beverly Hills. Grandpa was 75 and Jac was 15! We gave Jac a Minolta camera (of which, he earned most of it). He took pictures at the restaurant including a picture of his salad at 12 inches away. It looks like a picture in McCall's magazine.

We got home at 1:30 a.m. and got up at 5:30 a.m. to catch a plane for Oakland for Barbara Gibson's daughter's wedding at 11:00 a.m. at Orinda near Walnut Creek. Made it at 10 minutes to 11. Went to the reception in Danville and then slept 2 hours in our motel and then went to the Gibson's house for the afternoon and evening. Came home Sunday in time for Tom Brown's birthday party at their house. Lots of Sierra Madreans at the wedding. We came home with the Poolmans on the same flight.

I got a beautiful card from Jim to Jac and me. A painting of bamboo on the cover and inside a poem he wrote:

Choon Chun City
Kangwon Province, Korea
August 1971

Sitting on the hillside crowded
with green, growing things
Looking across the valley and
the uncountable tiny
paddies tall with rice
Slightly dizzy with full Summers'

> heavy sweet breath
> Thinking of home, but really
> Of the people there.
> Happy Birthdays Mom and Jac!

His last letter was to Jac for his birthday—just one sheet telling of his four weeks at Choon Chun taking a language course in Korean with forty other Peace Corps Volunteers. It is vacation time for the students so they are meeting in a very fancy girls' school, St. Somebody's near the top of Korea next to the U.S. Army base. There is a swimming pool on the base and a theater with American pictures. They study five hours a day and then they parade down to the base to go swimming. There are seventeen pianos in the school. He had brought his music, so he is playing two hours a day. A new friendship with the piano as he put it. He said it is really like a vacation as they have beds to sleep in and plumbing.

John played piano his first night at Villa Frascati Sunday night; the first few hours dragged because he was so nervous. But the last couple, until 2 a.m. went by fast as he got used to it. He made $50; $40 wages and $10 in tips.

Jean (my cousin) and I might go next Saturday night if we could find someone to go with us. Jon said the people are a little strange that frequent the place, so we don't want to go alone. Wish Tom was eighteen-the new law would let him go in.

Jean is coming Saturday to stay while Jimmy is in Hawaii. I work at the hospital Saturday, so I really won't even have one day to myself.

Two years later:

May 7, 1973

Dear Mom and Les (still traveling)

Your letter took a week to get here so thought I wouldn't have time to answer in Maryland. Mail is getting slower and slower. Jim's letters take 8 days now instead of 4.

I finally heard from him. He said he is busy, at fever pitch, but really enjoying it. He's teaching teachers. I received a darling letter from one of his students (from Korea) in a little rural town who teaches at Middle School. I don't think Jim knew he wrote it. He said Jim told him I advised Jim to go to Korea and he wanted to know why I advised him to go there instead of other "more charming places". It was a darling letter and very complimentary of Jim.

The schedule we sent to Jim is fine with him. He can meet us Friday, Sept. 28 at 11 a.m. in Seoul, and can go to Japan for the wedding.

Will write again to Illinois.

(My Mom and Les and Jimmy's brother Tom's mother-in-law Irene and I visited Jim in Korea and went with him after to Japan for a wedding of Jim's friend Yuki (from Stanford) in Shimizu, Japan. Jim went back to Korea and we four went on to Hong Kong, Taiwan, Thailand and Singapore. Another letter from me to my Mom:

June 8, 1973

Dear Mom and Les,

I planned to write yesterday or today--but now it is 2:45 and the first moment the house has been empty--and I have this feeling this quiet will be short lived. Tony has been camping at a camp at Santa Barbara for a week with his class. Tommy works from 4-11 six days a week at the Italian restaurant, not Monday which means he is here all day plus all his friends and loud records. Where are those quiet days when they used to go to school and Mom had some time to herself?

Jon has been baking an ice cream angel food cake which he is taking to the Arboretum as his goodbye gift and thank you to the staff. Yesterday I went to the Arboretum for coffee and doughnuts with the research department prior to his showing them the projects he had been working on. They are mostly doctors in biology or botany doing research there.

They were quite impressed with his work and encourage him to go after his doctorate. One man, a Doctor Ineri, told me, on the side, that Jon was very talented--the most observant person he had ever worked with. Dr. Chou (a Chinese) invited him to give the group a seminar when he returns in the Fall on anything he would like to do.

Tom is doing well at Dino's--making between $25 and $30 a day in tips and pay. Jac is studying for finals next week.

Sheba (**dog**) and the cats are shedding, and the weather has been in the 90's and smog alerts. Be glad you are where it is clear. Lots of love to you and the relatives. Ginny and crew.

(Two years later Mom and Les are still traveling and we had moved from our little tract house to the big house. I had dreams of a house with many bathrooms and it did come to pass!)

Thursday, Sept. 25, 1975

Dear Mom and Les,

Today I am finally doing the washing for the first time since before the wedding. (This was the wedding of my father-in-law who married Garnet after his wife Mimi passed away at 69 years old. Our backyard was about a hundred feet deep with a badminton court at the bottom and a swimming pool, a perfect place for a wedding and we had four or five while we lived there, friends and family.)

Back to my letter: *Things should return to normal (what's that???) by next week. The wedding was a big success--about 150 people from San Diego to San Jose and Hawaii. Everything looked beautiful. Abbey Rents put down imitation lawn on the badminton court and two yellow and white canopies over the buffet table. The tables were covered with yellow tablecloths and yellow daisies in the middle. We had everybody seated and could have squeezed another 30 or 40, I think.*

It seemed like the hottest day of the year, but it wasn't. The mercury has been climbing ever since--today 105. And as you can guess, I spent most of my time watering the lawns. My water bill for two months was $123 and that came before the hot spell. Of course, a lot of that was from putting in new lawns and flower beds. We planted three lawns and one of them wouldn't come up. We planted it three times.

The vegetable garden is still producing more than we can eat; beautiful cantaloupe, tomatoes, eggplant and four kinds of peppers, three very hot! Lots of green beans and our second crop of corn is 14 inches high. Nobody can get lids to can tomatoes. Rosemary made ten jars of chili sauce and gave me 3. Maxine canned green tomato pickles. I tell everyone they have to give me ten percent of their production for furnishing the tomatoes.

Tony's team won their first game. We couldn't go as we had to practice for the wedding. Betty Argy was "wedding director". Jon played a tiny organ on the veranda and Betty signaled Garnett and me on the terrace. The two Jim's and Mike (the minister) came through the basement bedroom door, and we came down the stairway. I was matron of honor and Jimmy was best man.

We had a dance floor put on the brick patio with a Yugoslavian band on the veranda in back of the garage. Luckily, that area is shaded in the afternoon. Did lots of circle dancing. Timmy Nickoloff from San Diego told me in the reception line that this was the best wedding he had ever attended. I told him to wait until his own!

Surprisingly, Garnett was shaking during the ceremony—I could see her bouquet shivering. I was remarkably calm, trying to keep the perspiration from running down my face. I kept saying to myself, keep cool!

Actually, I enjoyed the proceedings as though I was an observer. Having it catered, removed the pressure the last day.

I had better get this on the way or you will never get it before you move on. Tell Betty and family "hi".

Tommy will be leaving for Steamboat, Colorado, probably before you get home. He thinks he and a friend are going to run a Mexican Restaurant there!! See you in a few weeks. Love to you both. Ginny Lee

Chapter Ten

Letters are an interesting way of looking into the past. My mother found two letters in a museum in Minnesota that were almost falling apart. The first was written from California by my Great Great Grandfather's brother, James T. Lowry in 1851:

Scotts River, California.   July 10, 1851

My dear brother,

T. H. Adams has just arrived in the mines from Oregon and brought out my letters. One from you. And one from Father and one from Theop. Maybe I was glad to see them and thus to hear from you all but I was sorry to hear that you could not probably come out to Oregon this summer and now first if you can, come out by isthmus this winter.

I think you could get a place with the Surveyor General. Hank Adams got acquainted with him and engaged a place for him and me, expecting to be back from the mines in time, but as I did not come, he threw it up, but is confident we can get employment most of this summer and for this reason the Surveyor General didn't bring anyone out with him except his old surveyor. Nothing can be done this summer at the business except running the base and the meridian lines. All the sub-divisions are to be run next summer. Therefore, there will be a place for axmen, chain sawers, assistants, surveyors, also clerks & in the general post office. This he expects to find in Oregon and I am confident if you are here in time, anytime by the middle of March you can get a place. But if you can't, there are plenty of other stations I can get you into.

In your letter you speak of settleing yourself getting married and this is all well enough, but I think you had much better spend a year in the western country first in order to restore you to perfect health. If you don't make a cent, you will be amply rewarded in the renewal of your health. You will not lose any of the relish for refined society, nor will you lose any of your taste for the ladies in particular, nor your ability to gratify by amusing or exciting incidents.

Therefore, by all means come. Come by the isthmus. Leave New Orleans as early as the first of March and be sure to come on a steamer, at least on the Pacific. There is not certainty in sail vessels at that season when bound up. I haven't written any letters to you lately for I had hoped you had left Cave Hill and was by this time at the South Pole or Pacific. As it is, I will continue to write to you frequently until I see you. I hope you will also write regularly to me.

I am now out in the wildest country ever known to white man. It is about 200 miles to Shasta City, the nearest settlement in California, about 250 miles to the Umpjina Valley to the north. I suppose I am about 40 miles from the ocean on Scotts River, a branch of the Klamath. Trinity, Salmon, Scott and Shasta rivers are all branches of the Klamath, all emptying into it from the south. It is nearly 150 miles to the ocean by course of the rivers. I am not certain if I am in Oregon or California. I suppose I am near the line.

These mines were discovered late last fall. There are wild hostile Indians all around us. We **have** had two or three wars with them since I came here 2 months ago. Whenever the Indians get too troublesome, we raise a company of 25 to 200 volunteers and off we go, thrash around a while, kill a few, burn a few shanties and captivate a few squaws and come home and go to work.

The squaws are very wild at first and have to be guarded all the time, but in a little time by some kind of mesmeric influence they become so tame they won't go away. They bear the captivity with commendable resignation.

I left Oregon City March 3rd, arrived in Shasta diggings about the last of the month. I worked there about six weeks and made some two hundred dollars. Then I came over here and went to work. And after sinking several holes (one 42 feet) I made nothing. I got a share in a river claim, and we have dug 100 yards long and 8 feet deep, moved many rocks that weighed over a ton. Of course, I made nothing at this. We will be ready to turn the river in 2 weeks and then we expect to find a mule load.

I am in the company with a Dr. from Missouri in the practice of medicine. We have made about $1200. I have got my name up for a great surgeon, having performed several operations with success. When I leave here I will go to San Francisco and then to Oregon or to the Sandwich Islands (Hawaii).

Theop in his letter is very anxious we should all meet at Father's in July next summer. It would be a great pleasure to me but I can't promise for it is very uncertain where I will be. If I don't make a raise here I will spend next summer in Oregon or the Sandwich Islands. I think in Oregon, but no matter where I am I will always keep you informed of my whereabouts and my prospects. Write to me as before to Oregon City and I will find some means of getting the letters. I have here to send my letters by private conveyance to Oregon or Cal. to get them to the P.O. I make it a point to write to some of Father's family about once in 3 weeks, but I fear many of my letters never reach the P.O. However, I will keep writing. My health since I have been here has been good. I will weigh about 155 lbs. There will not be such sickness here this summer I think. The water is good and the weather cool, but if there is, I will open a hospital and go it indeed. I am in for anything I can make profitable.

I don't know that I will make a big raise, but I hope and expect to do something. But mining is the most uncertain of all lotteries, but I came here with no expectation of making much and shall not be grievously disappointed if I don't make anything. I let nothing fret me. I don't know any miners that make it as coolly as I do.

The Oregon fever is raging in Putman and Vermillion Counties. Mr. and Mrs. Moore <u>talk</u> only talk of going. Father and all the family are somewhat excited on the subject. Now if Father would sell his farm and effects for 1000 dollars, he could come easy enough. I would go back anytime and pilot him across.

The winters in Oregon are at least as mild as they are in Tennessee, and it is the cold winters in

Indiana that operate against Father's health. It would be also much better for Theop's health and Nancy's health and indeed for all the family, but I must close. Be sure to write to me. Give my love to your true lady and all the friends. I shall perhaps stay here until next October. Direct as before to Oregon City.

   I remain as ever your Brother
     James T. Lowry

The following excerpt was written by the sister of my great grandmother. The dateline was Sumner, Minnesota, dated September 3, 1858.

  I attended a wedding while at Cousin James. Mary Ann was married at a fair of the ladies sewing society. They were married just before supper and everyone was taken by surprise. She went to the fair as if nothing was going to happen and took an active part in receiving the guests and helping around until about the time for supper when she and her bridesmaids slipped upstairs where they had their clothes locked up in readiness and presently Mr. Dukes and his groomsmen are missing.

About the time they were ready to make their appearance Cousin James called the house to order and said they would have a few remarks from Rev. Mr. Adams of Traverse de Sioux. Adams stepped forward and commenced making some remarks and people, preparing themselves for a long speech, when the wedeners stepped in and he stopped immediately and performed the ceremony. You never saw such a surprised assembly in your life. There would not have been a greater change had there been a thunder bolt. They had a table set for 95 and it was filled three times. They had a splendid supper and ice cream and bride's cake passed around after supper.

(And I thought I had a big wedding!)

On our way home from Mankato, we had to come through the Indian Reservation which was very interesting to me as I had never been near an Indian. We had to carry our provisions with us and camp out.

The first nite we camped on the banks of the Le Seur and there were thick woods all around us. We made up a good fire and just had commenced eating when we heard the Indians coming. They had been to Mankato and were quite merry--- whooping and hollering, singing and presently an Indian came up followed by two squaws and they all squatted down on the ground around the fire and the Indian asked for bread. Father gave each a good large slice and they seemed well pleased and they all drank some whiskey which the men carried and sat about an hour smoking and laughing, talking and singing. Then they deemed it prudent to leave, the squaws when they arose to go came up to me and put their hands to have a shake. I did not know what they meant at first besides I felt a little afraid of them, but I shook hands with both of them.

They were dressed in true Indian style with blankets, moccasins, leggings and beads around their necks. One of them was very good looking.

That same nite after we were all asleep, there were five great big fellows came up to the wagon and called for whiskey, then they asked for tobacco and father gave them all a quid apiece and they went away singing. We could hear them for half an hour afterwards. They have such great big voices.

Well, I will tell you more adventure. We passed through villages. They make very queer looking houses out of bark and reeds with a hole through the top for the smoke to go out.

When we came to Big Cobb river we got stuck in the mud and could not get out. We worked for about an hour and could not make the wagon budge an inch, and we were about to give up in despair when a party of Indian hunters came up and Father asked one of them to help. So, the old fellow came up and examined the wheels and laid down his bundle and waded right into the water up to his waist and lifted the front wheel up out of the mud and waded around and took the tongue and he and another fellow with little assistance from Lizzie and father and pulled it through.

When they got ready to hitch the oxen, the big Indian turned to Lizzie and said "Squaw, go get oxen" and Lizzie started off like she was used to it. In the meantime, I was on the other side of the stream all alone surrounded by about a dozen Indians for I had to watch the load which we had to take out of the wagon.

But I will have to close tho I haven't written half what I want to. But my fingers ache for this is my second letter for this evening and besides the candle is most out and there is not another one. Now, do both of you write. I know you haven't much time but a letter from you does us all so much good.

We have made about 10 gallons of sugar cane molasses. Ann writes to me about everybody I know. Give my love to all the enquiring friends and kiss the little ones for me.

Your affectionate sister, Felicia

P.S. I forgot to say anything about marrying for if I was married you would like to know it. Well, I am not decidedly. And do not expect it before I see you again. I feel very much concerned about Julia for fear she may be snapped up one of these days. I am ashamed of this letter. But there goes my candle and I am in the dark. Goodbye, F.L.

The Julia who Felicia is concerned about was my great grandmother who did marry my Great Grandfather Clark Workman Seeley. I thought it interesting that their two oxen were named Tom and Jerry.

My mother's father, Otto Peter Schmidt was very patriotic and proud that he never missed voting in elections. His first vote for president was for William McKinley in 1896. You might get a kick out of his letter dated April 10, 1961. He was 88 years old at that time.

Honorable John F. Kennedy
Washington, D.C.

Dear Mr. President:

I beg the privilege of intruding on your official time, but first of all I wish to say that I am an old-time Republican and voted for Dick Nixon; however, you are **PRESIDENT OF THE UNITED STATES OF AMERICA**, and I trust you will use your best judgment and that you will be successful in administering the affairs of state for the people in general, and not just for the few who might demand special favors for their contribution to your election, for everybody who voted for you did just as much as any other one.

Before further comment, I wish to say I well remember the election of Grover Cleveland, first term, and all the elections, since my first vote was for William McKinley, so my comments are based on events that happened in my lifetime. Former President Woodrow Wilson permitted himself to be dragged off to France to help write the first World War treaty, and it cost him his life.

Let me say now that I had a neighbor, born in Germany who came to this country about 1885, and when he saw the headlines in the daily paper that President Wilson was going to France, he made this remark: "He is a dumb mule; they will dine him, wine him, entertain him with nice women,

And they will give him a dose of slow-acting poison, and in 6 months he will be dead."

Further commenting, he said, "The English ambassador in Washington is the top man in England, and the aim is to get the U.S.A. entangled in World affairs, so we will furnish them men and money to fight their wars."

No president before Wilson left the U.S.A. during his term of office, and I beg to suggest that you do not permit yourself to be induced to go to some out of the way place to confer with anyone regardless of whom, for if they want our help, let them come here asking for it.

You have every advantage by remaining in your office and telling your official family what to say and do. You need not worry about your enemies; you know who they are, but keep a close check on your friends, for you know that the Lord and Master was betrayed by his followers; people have not changed.

I trust you will keep this in confidence as I do not want to become involved in State affairs. Please do not surrender your advantage by being enticed to leave the confines of the United States--stay close to Washington and keep your powder dry.

Wishing you the help of every good American in your efforts to administer the affairs of state strictly in line with the Constitution, I am

                Sincerely yours,
                Otto P. Schmidt
                244 Atlantic Ave.
                Long Beach 2, Calif.

Chapter Eleven

How often have you been tempted to write a letter to the editor? It is everyone's privilege. In 1993 I wrote the following letter which was published in the Atlanta Journal Constitution entitled: Yams can make life sweeter:

I will be 70 years old in August, raised five sons and breezed through menopause, thanks to a little story told to me by my doctor. He said a team of doctors went to Mexico to discover why the women in a particular area seemed to pass through menopause with no problems and learned their primary diet was sweet potatoes.

These doctors started a company called Syntex, which made hormones out of yams, and the company became a giant on the New York Stock Exchange. At age 45, I started eating yams about three times a week. Whether this was the reason or not, I can't say; however, I had no hot flashes or any other problems. I still eat yams regularly in the hopes that those same hormones will aid in keeping my bones healthy.

My husband and I walk most every day and at age 54 we took up golf and snow skiing. Every doctor I have gone to has tried to put me on a hormone program, suggesting dire results if I don't take his advice. I still have all my insides and feel that the change was a natural function, and the end of menstruation was certainly welcome.

Your series "Hormones: the hot debate" said it is estimated as many as 50 percent of menopausal women in California have promoted this unnatural treatment which also involves repeated mammon-grams and pelvic exams, keeping their patients returning regularly.

My advice to women nearing menopause is eat sweet potatoes several times a week, take a walk every day and let nature take its course.

Once in a while, I get riled up and write to the editor to get something off my chest.

A letter from 1964 to the Pasadena Star News:

Dear Editor:

In reference to "Vent" on November 19. As one of the majority who "Van Dyke" claims put her head in the sand and did not see that the federal money for urban renewal would be withheld as a result of the "Yes" vote on Proposition 14, I maintain that you, sir, are much more guilty of putting your head in the sand.

Our whole society has become morally stagnant and lazy because of the continuing encroachment of government into our private lives. We used to be a nation of people who **EARNED** money received and a large part of the remuneration was pride in knowing that a job was well done.

With the Federal Government handing out money for such things as urban renewal, not only are people getting something for nothing, but many people are getting nothing for something. Why should a person in Montana pay taxes so that the city of Los Angeles can have a nice backdrop for their civic center. Should this not be the fruit of a city working for its own beautification? If the city cannot afford such a project yet, it should wait until it can. This urban renewal is just another way the Federal Government can get its hands into local government.

I say the best thing that resulted from the passage of Proposition 14 was to tell Uncle Sam, "We'd rather do it for ourselves."

The saddest thing of all is that our children are growing up in this "Great Society" where *receiving benefits is a way of life and* **EARNING** *what one receives is of little importance.*

Virginia Nickoloff

This is even truer today with a large part of our citizens not working at all!

In January 1997 there was an article in the paper with a London date line:

LONDON (AP) Her children's marriages didn't last, but hers did and Queen Elizabeth II is inviting **other** long married couples to a 50th anniversary bash. The Queen on Monday invited other couples married in 1947 to apply for the 4,000 invitations to her July 15 party in the palace gardens. Applications accompanied by a marriage certificate must be in by Feb. 14.

Long marriages are a feature of all walks of life and the garden party will give the queen and the duke an opportunity to meet people from a wide range of life experiences," a palace spokeswoman said.

Since Jimmy and I shared the same 50 years of "wedded bliss", I wrote a letter to the Queen with the help of a British friend of mine.

January 24, 1997

TO HER BRITANNIC MAJESTY
QUEEN ELIZABETH II

Your Majesty:

An article pertaining to Your Majesty's celebration of Her 50th Wedding Anniversary appeared in our local newspaper, The Times Georgian. A Palace spokeswoman said: "Long marriages are a feature of all walks of life and the garden party will give the Queen and the Duke an opportunity to meet people from a wide range of life experiences."

On February 16, 1947, my husband James Nickoloff and I were married in Los Angeles, California. He was a Naval Air Force pilot in World War II and returned to college after we were married. Four sons later, he graduated from law school. Our fifth and last son was born in 1959.

We raised our boys in Sierra Madre, a small town in California where we resided almost thirty years. Sierra Madre is two miles long and one mile wide nestled in the foothills. Its charm must have captured the hearts of some British subjects because a British Home was established there in

1931 providing a residence for elderly persons of British Commonwealth birth or parentage and sponsored by the Daughters of the British Empire in the United States of America.

We often attended their annual June fair and the fall "In-Gathering". A large portrait of Your Majesty hangs in the Salon. It was like a little bit of England in our midst. Eventually young British couples settled there also and introduced soccer to our small boys.

Several times over the years, the British Home has been honored by visits from Princess Margaret and Princess Alexandra and on one occasion, Prince Philip was in California for the Olympic Games in Los Angeles. His Royal Highness was presented with "Victory's Gate," a bronze equestrian sculpture by Michael Wilson, a friend of one of our sons.

Our eldest son, James, now 48 years old, did a science fair project when he was fourteen years old which involved requesting an ounce of soil from each state in the United States and places all over the world, including Alice Springs, Australia, Durban, South Africa, and Swindon, England. A neighbor was surprised to receive a clipping from her family in Swindon which announced: "An ounce of Swindon goes to the U.S.A.!

For the last six years, we have resided in a small suburb of Atlanta, Georgia. Amazingly, one of our neighbors of British descent is a member of the Atlanta Chapter of the Daughters of the British Empire. Each year she has invited me to their annual luncheon which is a fund raiser for the other British Home in Texas.

Perhaps Your Majesty would be interested to meet an American couple who shared those same fifty years of marriage. I am enclosing a copy of our marriage certificate. We would be honored to be considered for an invitation to Your Majesty's Celebration on July 15, 1997.

Jimmy promised if we are invited, we will go!

We soon received an answer from Buckingham Palace dated March 1997:

Dear Applicant,

I am commanded by The Queen to thank you for your recent letter concerning the Garden Party to be given by The Queen and The Duke of Edinburgh on Tuesday, 15th July 1997, for couples who were married in 1947, as part of the celebration to mark the Golden Wedding of Her Majesty and His Royal Highness.

I regret to say you are ineligible to apply for this occasion as The Queen is not the Head of State of your country. Indeed, in view of the heavy demand, it will not be possible to invite every eligible couple wishing to attend as only a total of 4,000 can be invited.

However, Her Majesty was interested to learn of your anniversary and hopes that you will much enjoy your own celebrations.

I am sorry to send you this disappointing reply,

Yours, sincerely,

    (an unreadable signature)
    State Invitations Assistant
    Lord Chamberlains' Office

In other words: You are not one of us.

Another missive received with the BUCKINGHAM PALACE letterhead in gold:

The Lord Chamberlain presents his compliments and thanks you for the enclosed attachments in support of your application to attend the Golden Anniversary Garden Party, which are returned for your safe keeping.

Queen Elizabeth's mother lived to 104. The Queen lost her husband Prince Phillip in 2021 and she passed away in 2023 at age 96 well-loved by her countrymen.

More recently I wrote to the Times-Georgian dated July 17-18, 2021, titled: Interested in the Truth about UFO's.

I am four years older than Mickey Mouse: I was 22 when I married in 1947. During the war years, housing construction was at a standstill so my husband and I couldn't find a place to rent. We put a deposit down on an apartment building that was under construction. During the six months (February to August 1947) we waited to move in, we lived with my husband's parents in Los Angeles.

One day, my mother-in-law and I were in their backyard when we looked up and saw a flying saucer just above the telephone poles. It hovered silently and moved on. We looked at each other and said, "What was that? We expected to find out in a newscast, but nothing was ever reported.

Since the disputed landing in New Mexico was in that time frame, I have no doubt that the

UFO we saw in Los Angeles could have traveled to Roswell, New Mexico in the blink of an eye.

No one in my family believes me. They think it is a joke. So, I, along with many others, anxiously await any information the government is finally going to report.

Ginny Nickoloff
Villa Rica, Georgia

The government is still not telling us anything about UFO's past or present. However, members of the Senate are pressuring the government to tell what they know about UFO's. Maybe someday my children will believe me.

I don't have a date for this letter I wrote to the Times Georgian:

It seems so sad that this country of "free souls" is still bogged down by racial unrest. My deceased husband was a lawyer in California, and he always wrote in the space for race: human. Nowadays, this is what we find: Which of the following best describes your ethnic background?
African American/Black
Asian or Pacific Islander
Caucasian/White

Hispanic
Some other background
Prefer not to say

Please tell me why this is necessary. All it does is separate us from each other. Why can't we be comfortable in our own skin and be a member of the human race? So many "Blacks" are voting for? So many Hispanics are voting against? If the statisticians would classify us all as people or humans on this planet, the separations, competitions, jealousies, hatreds, would certainly diminish and hopefully cease to exist in a more perfect world. We can be proud of our ethnic backgrounds, celebrate, enjoy and share our differences with each other, but let us not categorize us like a bunch of diverse animals. Let our well-known Southern hospitality offer a friendly nod and smile to passersby, especially if they look different from us. We are all members of the human race. Let's celebrate it!

Unfortunately, I do have to answer my own question. Working as a volunteer at Orthopaedic Hospital in Los Angeles, I had to ask the race question. My supervisor said that black people could have sickle cell anemia which would affect their treatment.

Another letter I wrote to the Times-Georgian dated December 28, 2019 entitled President Trump, keep cleaning the swamp.

The major problem with our government is our representatives and senators stay in office for years and years because they will never vote for term limits. It is up to us citizens to vote them out of office after eight years.

When President Trump offered to clean out the swamp in Washington, he set about doing that. Do the American people realize that Joe Biden has been milking the government purse for 36 years and now he wants additional benefits from a presidential term? Not only has he benefited, but so has his son.

They are part of the swamp. The fact that our president has not held office before is a big plus. He needs to bring in new blood by going after these old Government employees in the different departments. Everyone knows it is the president's job to select someone to represent us in each country, but I love the way he talks directly to the worlds' leaders—forget the go-betweens!

The President's tweets are his way of reaching the American people directly instead of through the biased news. Keep after that swamp, Mr. President.

In 1970, President Nixon signed a measure banning cigarette advertising on radio and television to take effect after Jan. 1, 1971. My husband sent the following letter to Time Magazine dated March 21, 1984:

>
> Mr. John A. Meyers, Publisher
> Time Magazine
> Time and Life Building
> Rockefeller Center
> New York, N. Y. 10020
>
> Dear Mr. Meyer:
>
> Time has a long history of excellence, and I am certain it will continue. However, it is my belief that Time could take a giant step in continuing and improving that tradition and showing the way to others in the media by engaging in self-denial of certain advertising revenue.
>
> Time should prohibit tobacco advertising in its magazine!
>
> I understand that the tobacco industry supplies much needed revenue for operating expense

and profit to those in your business. However, need alone is not reason enough to accept that money. There should be a consideration of your roll and duty to people.

I would hope and perhaps conjecture, it is possible to replace those tobacco ad-dollars with ad-dollars suggesting to your readers to purchase something of value instead of cigarettes resulting in the inevitable life-debasing effects of smoking.

When I see people smoking, see the advertisements, I hurt, and I have great sorrow for smokers, manufacturers, ad-people or anyone connected with the promotion of the use of tobacco. A religious person might say, "Forgive them for they know not what they do..." Me, I just hurt.

Sincerely,

James A. Nickoloff

P.S. If you care to respond in Time, please do. If you care to publish this, please do. It's free.

Here is the response from Time Magazine:

Time & Life Building
The Weekly News Magazine
Rockefeller Center

New York, 10020
John D. Walsh
Editorial Offices
April 24, 1984

Dear Mr. Nickoloff:

Thank you for letting us know how you feel about the inclusion of cigarette advertising in our pages. We respect your point of view, but our decision to accept this advertising is based on the fact that cigarettes are lawful terms of commerce. We therefore feel that the industry should not be denied the privilege—the privilege of all legitimate enterprise—of advertising openly. However, as you may be aware, in our Medicine section we take special care to report fully on the growing statistical and laboratory evidence linking cigarette smoking with cancer and heart and respiratory disease.

Sincerely,

(signature)

John D. Walsh

Rumors are spreading of the possible demise of the newspaper. That would break this old lady's heart. With great anticipation, I await the arrival of my daily newspaper, The Times Georgian. Even now, they have eliminated Mondays and only one paper for the two days of the weekend.

After checking the front-page news, I find the comic page. On the weekender I look forward to the Editorial page and also read the variety of columns written by members of our community. Are Daddy's still reading the funny paper to little children? That was a happy time in my childhood, crawling into bed with my Dad on Sunday morning with the Sunday funnies.

TV cannot replace the joy of reading a newspaper even though I watch the TV news. This past week, I watched the Arabian sheik and Netanyahu being interviewed. If Palestine, Israel, and Arabia would settle their differences, that would be a gigantic accomplishment in my lifetime! Unfortunately, war broke out soon after that interview between the Jews and Hamas. Horror has replaced peace.

Chapter Twelve

I'm happy Christmas letters are still being written. I have a Christmas letter my mother wrote:

CHRISTMAS 1996

Dear Family and Friends:

I'm still hale and hearty passing my 92nd mile-stone October 29. Three of my grandsons (Jon, Tony, Tom), Grand-daughter-in-law Dixie and great granddaughter Mary were at Virginia's house for my party. Grandson Jim sent a beautiful bouquet from Boston and Jac arrived from New Mexico a few days later.

I have been visiting my daughter for a couple weeks helping her husband Jim with some carpentering in their basement. He says he couldn't have done it without me!!

My youngest grandson Tony is living with me now which gives me peace of mind so I sleep good at night. He also takes me to the market and to doctor's offices. Thank goodness, the latter isn't needed very often as I am in good health.

Thanksgiving at Dixie and Tom's will be big. They are planning to open their ninth. La Paz restaurant in Alpharetta by Christmas. Alpharetta is north and east of me about 15 miles. In the meantime, I am enjoying eating at the newest one in Vinings, a little suburb of Atlanta, not too far from me.

My big trip this year was to the Seely Family Reunion in New Jersey. I flew by myself to Newark and the family met me. This was their 50th Annual picnic and I have been to the last 18.

Roy and Louise Seely are expected to drop in soon on their annual trek to Florida. I always enjoy having company and have plenty of room for any friends or family to visit.

Have a Merry Christmas and a good 1997. A new Century will be here before we know it.

Love,

Lola Virginia Cross

The following is my Christmas letter from 53 years ago:

Christmas 1971

Yuletide Greetings!

Twelve moons have passed since we last sent our Christmas greetings to friends near and far. Happily, new friends have enlarged out circle and together with old friends, keep the circle whirling and exciting.

1971 found only five Nickoloffs still residing at 311 San Gabriel Court as Jim and John set up their own pads—five thousand miles apart. Jim left on. January 18 for Korea and a two-year adventure serving in the Peace Corps. He is the only Westerner in the village of Andong where he assists the Korean English teachers at Andong Middle School. They had been teaching English for ten years, but could not speak the language. He has a good friend in Yi Yun Mu, his co-teacher, and on weekends meets other Peace Corps friends while traveling about visiting famous landmarks throughout the country. To quote a February letter. "Twenty-five straight meals with rice—and no end in sight. Thank God, I like it. In two years that's 2,190 meals of rice."

John is attending. Long Beach State, majoring in biology. He and two friends live in a beautiful apartment in Seal Beach. Piano is still his first love as he has rented one and is teaching three students to cover the rental cost. He enjoys cooking from scratch—even makes bread!

Tom is a senior at Pasadena High School and the proud owner of a set of wheels—a white Dodge Van. Varsity football has kept him so busy this fall, he hasn't had time to fix it up yet. The season ended last Friday night in the Rose Bowl *with the Pacific League Championship under their belt and two wins in C.I.F. finals; their record 9-2-1. Tom's hard tackles were a thrill for his family, devoted spectators who never missed a game—from Santa Monica to Redlands, including a two-hour down-pour in Santa Ana.*

(The Rose Bowl always reminds me of one of my scariest days. Sorry if I am repeating myself. Jimmy and I were at the Rose Bowl watching and filming Tom's game when I realized everyone was looking up behind me. Tony (12 years old) was climbing up one of the light towers. Jimmy ran up to get him to come down.

Watching the Rose Bowl game on TV this year, Tom and I checked out those tall lamp posts and thought of Tony. We always enjoy it when the cameras turn toward Sierra Madre and our beautiful Mount Wilson that rises 5,710 feet above our town and has an observatory on the top.

When Tony was about 9 years old, he told me he was going to run around our block. When I asked why, he said he was getting in shape for the 9-mile trail race up Mount Wilson that was happening the next day. Amazingly, he won for his age group!)

To continue my Christmas letter:

Jac, a tenth grader, is constantly embarking on some major project—usually in the electronic field. Of late, he has been making louder noises about setting up a darkroom in my bathroom as photography comes to the fore. He and his friend Ken built a Citizen Band radio and aircraft radio for Dad, and also blast us out of the house with stereo music (?). Baseball occupied spring and summer as Jac's All-Star team had a fantastic year and Jac won the batting crown with a .484 average.

Twelve-year-old Tony is our playboy: catcher for the Red Sox and now in the middle of the soccer season. He also organized the first flag football team at Ascension Parish School. Tony and school are getting on friendlier terms.

Mom and Pop had a vintage year. A wonderful trip to Hawaii in February to attend the twenty-fifth wedding anniversary of sister Nada and Newell had to be the high point. Pop boarded the 747 again in August and joined Newell and two other men friends on a sailing trip around Maui and Molokai—that's what dreams are made of! When Mom isn't sitting in the stands at some sporting event, she is involved with the Crippled Children's Guild and its many projects.

So that is the story of the Nickoloffs as another holiday season approaches. We send our *love and best wishes for a healthy, happy New Year.*

Jim and Ginny
Jim, John, Tom, Jac and Tony

Christmas 1992

Merry Christmas
Happy New Year

1992—the year of the **Big Fly** the **Big Move**, and the **Big Storm!**

Yes! the Glassair had its maiden flight on Ginny's birthday, August 25th! It was very evident there had been a "happening" when Ginny returned from golf to see a happy Jim smiling from ear to ear! Since then, Jim has put about 7 hours on the sleek little bird around the Apple Valley airport. He says it flies like a dream!

Yes! in late November we moved everything from Apple Valley to Villa Rica. The Apple Valley house is for sale; however, we plan to be there from January 10 until our nephew Kevin's wedding February 13 in San Diego.

Yes! the big tornado hatched a few miles from our house. Ginny took heed of the warnings and shut herself in a hallway in the basement with a book to read while Jim unpacked his clothes in the bedroom and watched the storm blow through, raising oceanlike waves on our lake! Even though the lights went out, Ginny stayed in the dark until it was all over (smart chicken!) After witnessing the damage, Jim may join her in the basement next time! (Seventeen trees went down in the front yard}.

All the Nickoloffs were in the same time zone. At Thanksgiving. Jac and his new bride were in Boston, but with Jon's first visit to Georgia, all the rest of us were at Grandma Lola's for Thanksgiving dinner (18 in all). As always, her turkey was the juiciest around.

Much to our delight, lots of Californians visited us here this year. We hope more of you will come on down and share some grits and cornbread in 1993! Have a Happy Holiday Season and keep jingling y'all!

Love,

Jim and Ginny

Chapter Thirteen

On January 2023, I was invited to a zoom meeting of the Parentis Foundation associated with *AARP,* a group of men and women who help young children who are slow learners. They are located in Southern California and invited me because I had written children's books. I was overjoyed to receive letters from the participants after the meeting, proving that letter writing is not dead yet!

One letter from Connie Simon, Santa Ana, California:

January 28, 2023

Dear Ginny,

I'm a tutor with Parentis Foundation and participated in the zoom meeting at which you spoke. I share your love of letter writing and traveling and wanted to thank you for sharing your travel adventures with all of us.

I'm sad about the loss of letter writing. I try to write to my grandkids, so they have the experience of the excitement of receiving something by mail.

I've learned about some family history when finding an old letter written in the last century that had been forgotten amongst my parents' things. Letters are so precious.

Hope you are able to celebrate your milestone birthday at the former Sir Francis Drake Hotel!

From Alicia Price, Laguna Niguel:

Jan. 23, 2023

Hello Ginny,

Thank you for presenting at our Coffee Chat meeting as part of our Life Long Learners Series.

It was delightful hearing about your books, travels and life experiences. It was inspiring.

I was impressed with your adventurous spirit and can-do attitude. I wish we could have visited longer.

I have a collection of hats and yesterday when I wore one of them, I thought of you. It has been a pleasure making your acquaintance.

Stay well and enjoy your upcoming Centennial Birthday celebration in San Francisco.

From Karen Campbell, Studio City

January 28, 2023

Hi Ginny,

My name is Karen, and I am one of the tutor volunteers for Parentis Foundation. I really enjoyed your presentation last week. You are such an inspiration. I was the one who shared the picture of the little girl in my mom's hat.

  Bless you, Karen

From Bonnie Gillespie, Santa Ana, CA
1-24-2023

Dear Miss Ginny,

  Thank you for joining us to share your amazing experiences with us. I immediately ordered your book on Egypt. It is delightful.

  I taught in Saudi Arabia for 4 years in the 80's and always encourage young people to travel prior to getting settled in their jobs. You are such an inspiration for others. I'm trying to convince my husband to take on a tour to Africa. Is your lady in Santa Barbara still leading tours?

  May you continue to be blessed with your travels.

  Warm Regards,
  Bonny Gillespie

From Linda Klasky, San Juan Capistrano.

January 21, 2023

Dearest Ginny,

I just wanted to tell you how much I enjoyed hearing of your travels and stories. I especially liked the story about the horse and zebras. What an experience!

Thank you for sharing your books and telling us about your plans for your 100th birthday! I haven't written a letter in a long, long time, but I do wear a baseball hat in the sun!

Thank you again!

Hats were brought up during the call, or should I say the lack of hats in this modern age. In the 1940's, men and women wore hats whenever they went out. If you watch old movies, notice that men took their hats off when they entered an elevator with women aboard. That's just one of the gentlemen niceties that are disappearing or have disappeared. I have noticed watching old movies that in the early days, even in America, people bowed to each other, smaller than a real curtsy to royalty. More of a nod.

What I miss are the hat and shoe stores that were in every town. I loved going in a hat store, sitting down in front of a mirror and having the salesgirl bring hats to try on. It was a part of the fun of being a girl. Come to my house sometime and I'll show you my hats that I keep to show my granddaughters (including my wedding hat). My mom and I had our wedding hats made by a hat maker. Mine is pink feathers. In the next picture, Jimmy and I are leaving the reception hall where we had dinner, dancing and cutting the wedding cake.

Jimmy bought his Stetson at a men's hat store.

From Janice Freschette, Laguna Hills:

Dear Ms. Ginny,

On behalf of myself and The Parents Foundation team, we want to thank you for joining us on our weekly Lifelong Learner Coffee Chat! You are truly an inspiration to all of us.

Thank you for reminding us all that living to plan, and planning to live are vital. Thank you for sharing stories of your travel adventures and your family adventures as well!

We look forward to hearing all about your trip to San Francisco for your 100th B-Day! Please stay in touch and let us know when your next book is published.

Warm Regards,
Janice and the Parentis Foundation Team

From Sheri Yee, Mission Viejo:

Jan 21, 2023

Hi Ginny,

Thank you so much for speaking to us at Parentis/**AARP** reading tutors coffee chat via zoom. It was so inspiring to hear of your travels.

I have not rode an elephant, but have swam with dolphins in Hawaii.

I do ipad painting as a hobby in my retirement from graphic design. I enjoy playing cards with my mom and auntie who are both in their 80's.

I am happy to hear you are in good health and remaining active!

Blessings to you and your family,
Sheri Yee

Speaking of card playing, I have played in bridge groups for years and still play bridge once a week. I also love to play hearts with the boys and Scrabble with Jessie and Tom playing the fun rules invented by son Tony. Good for the brain cells!

From Joi Defoe, Huntington Beach:

Jan 20, 2023

Hi Ginny, I very much enjoyed listening to your stories about your rich expansive life. You are quite an inspiration.

My love of traveling began late in life. My daughter, Sierra, who is now 28 is my favorite travel buddy. She got the bug in high school when her classmates went to France (French class). She took full advantage of the travel abroad option in college and also while getting her Masters in Public Health. Since then we have been to the following places together: Nice, France, Mauritius, Tahiti, and Morea, Copenhagen and Sweden, New Zealand and without her I've been to London twice and to various states in the U.S. My future travel plans: going to New Zealand (again and where she lives) and then to Portugal in the fall with my husband.

    I want to wrap it up by saying thank you. Thank you for inspiring so many other people and especially for writing children's books. In my mind, reading is everything and without it, life is a small, small place.

    I wish you safe Travels and good health.

    All the best,

    Joi

From Gwen Ginocchio, Laguna Woods
1/26/2024

Dear Ginny,

We thoroughly enjoyed your visit via Zoom. The volunteer Tutors are a great group and I'm sure we were all inspired by your sense of adventure, your creativity and enthusiasm for life. Thank you so much for sharing. I've visited your website and will look up your books on Amazon. Keep on keepin' on!

Much admiration,
Gwen Ginocch

From Nan Liebsack   Jan 20, 2023

Dear Ginny,

Thank you for joining our coffee chat last week, for the Parentis Foundation. I am a brand-new volunteer with the organization and thoroughly enjoyed listening to the chat.

I am glad you are doing journals on your trips and writing books on your experiences. And exposing your grandchildren to such adventures is wonderful.

I am not much of a traveler, but the one trip I took to Paris some years ago, certainly opened my eyes to a much bigger world. I think it gives you so much more depth and understanding when you travel outside of your own little world. But sadly, I didn't experience the pinch....lo!

Your attitude toward life is amazing. You are an inspiration for all of us.

Good luck with getting your latest book published. I look forward to seeing it on the bookshelves this year.

With best regards, Nan Liebsack (an old school letter writer)

To explain the "pinch," Nan is referring to my being pinched in the butt when I was in a crowd in St. Peters Basilica in the Vatican while the Pope and the Cardinals were entering under a canopy. Only in Italy! What made this so ridiculous is when you enter the basilica, on your right is the beautiful sculpture of the Pieta by Michelangelo. Sort of like going from the sublime to the ridiculous.

With this bit of humor, I leave you with the hope that letters don't disappear completely from our world.

           Very truly yours,
           Ginny Nickoloff

P.S. I love you!

Acknowledgements

A special thanks to my son
Jim who also saved letters
and
to Robert McCleary, who helped
me with my pictures

and to my dear editor, Elyse Wheeler

www.ingramcontent.com/pod-product-compliance
Lightning Source LLC
Chambersburg PA
CBHW070046080526
44586CB00013B/928